I0235412

THE TOWER OF THE WINDS IN ATHENS

THE TOWER OF THE WINDS IN ATHENS

Greeks, Romans, Christians, and Muslims: Two Millennia of Continual Use

PAMELA A. WEBB

American Philosophical Society Press
2017

Memoirs
of the
American Philosophical Society
Held at Philadelphia
for Promoting Useful Knowledge
Volume 270

ISBN-13: 978-0-87169-270-2

Library of Congress Cataloging-in-Publication Data

Webb, Pamela A., author.
The Tower of the Winds in Athens : Greeks, Romans, Christians, and Muslims : two millennia of continual use / Pamela A. Webb.
p. cm. — (Memoirs of the American Philosophical Society, held at Philadelphia for promoting useful knowledge ; Volume 270)
Philadelphia : American Philosophical Society, 2017
Includes bibliographical references and index.
LCCN 2017027792 | ISBN 978-0-87169-270-2 (hardback : alk. paper)
Tower of the Winds (Athens, Greece) | Sacred space—Greece—Athens. | Towers—Greece—Athens. | Athens, (Greece)—Religious life and customs. | Athens (Greece)—Buildings, structures, etc.
DF287.T68 W43 2017
725/.970949512—dc23

2017027792

Jacket and frontispiece: Views of the Tower of the Winds from the north with the Erechtheum on the Acropolis in the background (P. Webb).

WINNER OF THE 2016 JOHN FREDERICK LEWIS AWARD

To my grandchildren, Gracie and Jack Garofalo—
my inspiration personified.

What happens in the sky, in the air, on earth,
and on the sea is due to the wind.

Theophrastus (*De ventis* 1)

IN LOVING MEMORY OF WHITFIELD J. BELL

(1914–2009)

Librarian of the American Philosophical Society, 1966–1980

Executive Officer of the American Philosophical Society, 1977–1983

CONTENTS

ABBREVIATIONS

AA: Archäologischer Anzeiger

AJA: American Journal of Archaeology

AJP: American Journal of Philology

AM: Mitteilungen des Deutschen Archäologischen Instituts, Athenische Abteilung

AnnNYAcadSci: Annals of the New York Academy of Sciences

AR: Archaeological Reports (supplement to *JHS*)

ArchDelt: Archaiologikon Deltion

ArchEph: Archaiologike Ephemeris

ArchKorrBl: Archaeologisches Korrespondenzblatt

ArtBull: The Art Bulletin

ArtMed: Arte Medievale

AvP: Altertümer von Pergamon

BICS: Bulletin of the Institute of Classical Studies of the University of London

BSA: *Annual of the British School at Athens*

ByzZeit: Byzantinische Zeitschrift

CathEnc: The Catholic Encyclopedia

CCAM: Committee for the Conservation of the Acropolis Monuments

CIG: Corpus Inscriptionum Graecarum

Deltion: Deltion tēs Christianikēs Archaiologikēs Hetaireias

DOP: Dumbarton Oaks Papers

DOS: Dumbarton Oaks Studies

Eulimene: Studies in Classical Archaeology, Epigraphy, Numismatics and Papyrology

HEROM: Journal on Hellenistic and Roman Material Culture

Hesperia: Hesperia: The Journal of the American School of Classical Studies at Athens

HTS: HTS Teologiese Studies / Theological Studies

ISAW Papers: Institute for the Study of the Ancient World

IstMitt: Istanbuler Mitteilungen

IstMitt BH: Istanbuler Mitteilungen: Beiheft

JdI: Jahrbuch des Deutschen Archäologischen Instituts

JHA: Journal for the History of Astronomy

JHS: Journal of Hellenic Studies

Öjh: Jahreshefte des Österreichischen archäologischen Institutes in Wien

JRS: Journal of Roman Studies

J. Semitic Studies: Journal of Semitic Studies

J. Turkish Studies: Journal of Turkish Studies

Kernos: Kernos—Revue internationale et pluridisciplinaire de religion grecque antique

LIMC: Lexicon Iconographicum Mythologiae Classicae

MAA: Mediterranean Archaeology and Archaeometry

SEG: Supplementum epigraphicum graecum

Speculum: Speculum: A Journal of Medieval Studies

TechnolCult: Technology and Culture: The International Quarterly of the Society for the History of Technology

ZPE: Zeitschrift für Papyrologie und Epigraphik

PREFACE

I have come to think of this monograph as an accidental book. It grew—out of unplanned necessity—from what was to have been a five-page entry in a section of a catalogue covering monuments in Athens in a partially completed volume on Hellenistic architectural sculpture. Each of those entries includes a brief description of the architecture and discussion of the building's history. In the case of the Tower of the Winds, also known as the Horologion of Andronikos, confining my comments to a few pages proved to be a severe challenge in that this tall octagonal structure in central Athens is distinctive architecturally and performed a variety of functions over two millennia of active use.

As my research progressed, I accumulated a list of questions about the purposes the building served over the centuries whose answers were not directly apparent, even though published material relating to the monument is fairly extensive. I came to conclude that this was due to this Hellenistic edifice having been of interest chiefly to classical scholars who concentrated primarily on the building's Greek and Roman phases. Thus, the corpus of publications, consisting of a number of articles and two monographs, deals primarily with the classical monument in its Hellenistic form and Roman renovations carried out in the first century AD. The most important of these studies of the monument is *Der Turm der Winde in Athen* by Hermann Kienast, published in 2014. This volume provides a detailed analysis of the structure's architectural design and execution, and I am greatly indebted to the author for his comprehensive examination of the Tower's early centuries.[1]

How the building functioned over time, however, remains open to interpretation. While earlier publications supplied a sound foundation for my research, certain conclusions offered therein seemed to me to call for re-examination, and many questions regarding its later history remained unanswered. This led to a much more protracted process of inquiry than had been originally intended. Thus, as I read, examined, and analyzed the material, what had originally been planned as a catalogue entry grew from five to twenty-five pages. I decided that at that length it would have to be part of the book's appendix. As I wrestled with a number of additional questions, however, my

1. For a review of Kienast's monograph, see Webb (2015).

notes grew to fill forty pages, at which point I believed I had material suitable for a journal article. Unfortunately, the text did not encompass the entirety of the building's operative life and left unaddressed a number of problems that I thought might be resolved through more comprehensive study of the Tower as it functioned throughout Late Antique, Byzantine, and Ottoman Athens. By the time that was accomplished, the article ran to well over a hundred pages, and it became clear that the manuscript was not within the parameters set for length by scholarly journals. Consequently, the history of the monument analyzed herein, which spans two thousand years, imposed what was always going to be required—a comprehensive view and a diachronic approach to the subject presented in a volume dedicated solely to itself and to the entirety of its functional existence.

The resulting monograph addresses diverse issues from each of the monument's historical periods, including the following: Is it possible to identify the patron who supplied funds for the Tower's construction? In the Hellenistic and Roman periods, was the Tower only a horologion that housed some form of water-run device, or did it have a cultic and commemorative function as well? Is it possible to suggest how the building was used in Christian Athens, considering the paucity of historical and archaeological evidence from that period? Can the information regarding the Tower's function during the Ottoman phase be clarified and expanded?

Discussions regarding topics such as patronage and Greek religious cult are important for consideration by classical scholars. An additional goal, however, is to create greater awareness of and familiarity with the Tower of the Winds among scholars who concentrate on post-classical Athens and to make available in a single volume analyses of each of the building's periods of occupation. Investigations of classical monuments in the city generally have placed their greatest emphasis on the religious and civic structures on the Acropolis and in the Greek Agora, including the two most important buildings that continued in use from antiquity through the Ottoman periods—the Parthenon and the Erechtheum. In my opinion, the Tower of the Winds, which stood below these two monuments at the foot of the great hill's north side, should assume a more prominent place in investigations of Athens' classical and later history.

A great deal is known about most types of Greek buildings—temples, altars, stoas, theaters, and other religious and civic structures. Little physical evidence remains, however, of the architecture and implements that served the academic and scientific spheres of ancient life. The Academy is gone, as are the Lyceum, the libraries at Pergamon and Alexandria (and Alexandria's great lighthouse), Archimedes' celestial globes, and most other such impressive creations from the classical world. But the Tower of the Winds still stands, a tangible product of one of the many great mathematical and engineering minds of the Hellenistic period. Because this building survives, an extensive set of accurate vertical sundials has come down to us, the only known examples from antiquity. The physical structure and literary sources supply evidence of a figured weather vane that worked in coordination with the largest visual display of the winds from antiquity. Moreover, this is the earliest known verifiable permanent weather vane.

The water-run device from the interior of this monument may be long gone and its specific form resists identification, but remnants of the system that powered it provide proof of its size and complexity. Thus, this great octagon is a material connection to parts of the past that have largely disappeared. That the Tower was important to the intellectual life of Hellenistic and Roman Athens cannot be doubted. Defining its role in Byzantine Athens has been far more problematic. Evidence suggests, however, that this classical building when consecrated for Christian use may have served as a martyrium for the Apostle Philip.

My research has resulted in findings that lie along a broad range of confidence. Some I deem to be strongly supported by the evidence. Others are hypotheses that warrant serious consideration. A certain number are suggestions I regard as interesting to contemplate. Firm answers in many cases are elusive. In the process of analyzing problems posed by an equally perplexing monument—the Horologium of Augustus in Rome—Haselberger offers a constructive caveat that can also be applied to the Horologion of Andronikos in Athens: "The role of the monument as a *Gesamtkunstwerk* of astronomical science, monumental architecture, urban landscape design, theatrical spectacle, ideological propaganda, and political agenda is unparalleled. So are the risks and complexities of its investigation; simple solutions are not at hand."[2]

I wish to thank the National Endowment for the Humanities and the American Philosophical Society for grants that provided support for this research and allowed me the opportunity to travel to Greece to study monuments adorned with architectural sculpture, including the Tower of the Winds. The building was closed for a number of years, consequently during my first visit I was able to view it only from the exterior. Fortunately, the Tower was reopened to the public in the summer of 2016, and I was able to examine and photograph the interior at that time. I am also grateful for the support of the Department of Classical and Near Eastern Archaeology at Bryn Mawr College and its chairman, Peter Magee. The staff of the Rhys Carpenter Library at the college—Camilla Mackay, Jeremy Blatchley, and Del Ramers—supplied important assistance regarding written sources and visual images. I want to thank Elaine Beretz and Alicia Walker (Bryn Mawr College), Vasiliki Limberis (Temple University), and Brian Rose (University of Pennsylvania) for their valuable comments on an early version of the manuscript. As regards the final version, I am grateful for the many helpful comments and suggestions from Thomas Brogan (INSTAP Study Center for East Crete) and several anonymous readers. I am most appreciative of the support of Mary McDonald (director of publications at the American Philosophical Society) and the members of the APS publications committee. And finally, I am expressly indebted to

2. Haselberger (2014) 185.

Brunilde Ridgway who, whenever I found the effort consuming far too much of my time, urged me to carry on and complete the work.

Throughout my main text the appellations Octagon and Horologion are used interchangeably with the word Tower in order to reduce redundancy. They are capitalized to denote that they are intended as a name for the monument rather than solely as a specific description of its architectural form or as a definition of the building's function. An attempt has been made to apply the terms polytheist and pagan according to the historical context in which they appear, although the choice between them at times is ambiguous.

I have generally favored Latinized /Anglicized forms over Greek spellings for proper and common nouns. This was especially necessary in cases where there were variations of the same word in different historical periods (for example, Ariobarzanes of Kappadokia and Saint Basil of Cappadocia). Andronikos Kyrrhestes and the wind gods have been permitted to retain the Greek forms of their names throughout, however. There are other inconsistencies as well that I hope will be found to be tolerable.

THE TOWER OF THE WINDS IN ATHENS

INTRODUCTION

Few buildings have a history as long and complex as the Tower of the Winds, also known as the Horologion of Andronikos.[1] The operative life of this structure covers two millennia (second century BC to eighteenth century AD), three religions (classical polytheism, Christianity, and Islam) and four cultures (Greek, Roman, Byzantine, and Ottoman). A distinctive monument located to the north of the Acropolis in the area of the Roman Agora, it is a tall octagon lying on a north-south axis with a semicircular annex attached at its south side (Frontispiece; Ills. 1–5). The uppermost courses of the walls are adorned with a large sculptured frieze depicting eight wind gods. Each figure is identified by name—engraved into the molding above—and is located on the side of the building from which it blows. The Hellenistic building was both a weather station and a timepiece, providing ancient Athenians with meteorological and chronometric information through its weather vane atop the roof and sundials on its exterior walls. A system of channels and pipes, leading to and lying within and under the structure, indicates that it housed some type of water-run mechanism.

Two Roman authors, Vitruvius and Varro, provide the only descriptions of the Tower of the Winds from antiquity. In *De Architectura* 1.6.4–5, Vitruvius states:

> 4. Nonnullis placuit esse ventos quattuor, ab oriente aequinoctiali solanum, a meridie austrum, ab occidente aequinoctiali favonium, ab septentrionibus septentrionem. sed qui diligentius perquisierunt tradiderunt eos esse octo, maxime quidem Andronicus Cyrrestes, qui etiam exemplum conlocavit Athenis turrim marmoream octagonon et in singulis lateribus octagoni singulorum ventorum imagines excalptas contra suos quosque flatus designavit, supraque eam turrim metam marmoream perfecit et insuper Tritonem aereum conlocavit dextra manu virgam porrigentem, et ita est machinatus uti vento circumageretur et semper contra flatum consisteret supraque imaginem flantis venti indicem virgam teneret. 5. itaque sunt conlocati inter solanum et austrum ab oriente hiberno eurus, inter austrum et favonium ab occidente hiberno africus, inter favonium et septentrionem caurus, quem plures vocant corum, inter septentrionem et solanum aquilo. hoc modo videtur esse expressum uti capiat numeros et nomina et partes unde flatus certi ventorum spirent. quod cum ita exploratum habeatur, ut inveniantur regiones et ortus eorum sic erit ratiocinandum.

1. For an extended discussion of the Tower's early investigators, see Kienast (2014) 1–20.

4. Some have held that there are only four winds: Solanus from due east; Auster from the south; Favonius from due west; Septentrio from the north. But more careful investigators tell us that there are eight. Chief among such was Andronicus of Cyrrhus who in proof built the marble octagonal Tower in Athens. On the several sides of the octagon he executed reliefs representing the several winds, each facing the point from which it blows; and on top of the Tower he set a conical shaped piece of marble and on this a bronze Triton with a rod outstretched in its right hand. It was so contrived as to go round with the wind, always stopping to face the breeze and holding its rod as a pointer directly over the representation of the wind that was blowing. 5. Thus Eurus is placed to the southeast between Solanus and Auster: Africus to the southwest between Auster and Favonius; Caurus, or, as many call it, Corus, between Favonius and Septentrio; and Aquilo between Septentrio and Solanus. Such, then, appears to have been his device, including the numbers and names of the wind and indicating the directions from which particular winds blow. These facts being thus determined, to find the directions and quarters of the winds your method of procedure should be as follows. (trans. M. H. Morgan)

Varro, when describing his aviary at Casinum, writes in *De Re Rustica* 3.5.17:

Intrinsecus sub tholo stella lucifer interdiu, noctu hesperus, ita circumeunt ad infimum hemisphaerium ac moventur, ut indicent, quot sint horae. In eodem hemisphaerio medio circum cardinem est orbis ventorum octo, ut Athenis in horologio, quod fecit Cyrrestes; ibique eminens radius a cardine ad orbem ita movetur, ut eum tangat ventum, qui flet, ut intus scire possis.

Inside, under the dome of the rotunda, the morning-star by day and the evening-star at night circle around near the lower part of the hemisphere, and move in such a manner as to show what the hour is. In the middle of the same hemisphere, running around the axis, is a compass of the eight winds, as in the horologium at Athens, which was built by the Cyrrestian; and there a pointer, projecting from the axis, runs about the compass in such a way that it touches the wind which is blowing, so that you can tell on the inside which it is. (trans. W. D. Hooper and H. B. Ash)

Both authors focus particularly on the fact that the monument is adorned with eight sculptural representations of wind gods.[2] We are also informed that Andronikos of Kyrrhos was the builder.[3] Vitruvius refers to the structure as an eight-sided marble Tower. Varro calls it a horologion, a term that applies to both sundials and water clocks.

2. Four named winds was more common practice. Aristotle (*Meteorologika* 2.6.363a), followed by Theophrastus and other classical philosophers, however, lists twelve named winds, a system that may be the oldest, going back to the Babylonians and the Phoenicians.

3. Whether Kyrrhos is the city in Macedonia mentioned by Thucydides (2.100.4) or the city in Syria is not specified. Robinson's identification of Andronikos as a Macedonian astronomer who was also responsible for a marble sundial in the Sanctuary of Poseidon and Amphitrite on Tinos has been generally accepted. See Robinson (1943) 293, 297 n. 15; Etienne and Braun (1986) 195–96 and n. 472, 313 n. 56, pls. 168.4–5; Kienast (2014) 142–43. Corso (1997) 374, 400, believes Andronikos was from Kyrrhos in Syria.

Neither commentary includes a description of the building's interior, nor do they refer to the water-run mechanism.[4]

A stele inscribed with an Attic decree (*IG* II^2, 1035), dating to the Augustan period, likely provides a third reference from antiquity.[5] The decree lists various sanctuaries and public properties that had fallen into private hands. They were to be restored to public ownership and repaired at the expense of the state, and the sanctuaries were to be reconsecrated. Line 54 makes reference to the οικος of the man from Kyrrhos (οἰκίαν τὴν λεγομένην Κυρρήστου). Οικος has been taken by most scholars to mean "building," not "house," and the man from Kyrrhos as Andronikos.

Robinson rejects the idea that it is the Horologion to which line 54 refers, believing instead this was some other building connected with Andronikos. He concludes that the properties listed in *IG* II^2, 1035, which are grouped by geographic region, were all outside the city walls and that the οικος of the Kyrrhestian is listed with properties in the area of Mount Hymettus. Thus, Robinson suggests that the οικος is not the Tower of the Winds but instead is an observatory on Mount Hymettus used by Andronikos in making necessary measurements for the design of the scientific devices of the Horologion. Kienast also disputes that it is the Tower to which line 54 refers but for the following reasons: the word οικος is too general an appellation to be applied to such a significant monument, and it is doubtful that the structure was in need of significant repairs, even taking into consideration the invasion of Athens by the Roman general Sulla in 87/86 BC and the building's more than a century of use.[6]

The wording of the decree may be vague, but the commonly accepted conclusion that Andronikos' Horologion is named in the list cannot be dismissed. Culley's analysis of *IG* II^2, 1035, demonstrates that lines 53–57 refer to properties within the city of Athens; thus, he identifies the edifice in line 54 as the Tower of the Winds. The absence of Andronikos' name in conjunction with the building is not significant, for it seems quite plausible that those responsible for the compilation of the structures included in the decree might have used shorthand terminology similar to that found in Varro, who merely alludes to the architect as the Kyrrhestian (*fecit* Cyrrestes). Thus, it is reasonable to infer the following: the building listed in line 54 is the Horologion; at some point in the late Hellenistic period the monument had been transferred to

4. It is curious that this unusual and spectacularly interesting monument does not appear in the writings of other ancient authors, including Pausanias—although analyzing the omissions in the narratives of this second century travel writer can be a trying task. As a point of comparison, one need only ponder why he omits mention of the extraordinary sculptured frieze in his discussion of the Parthenon.

5. For analyses of the date and interpretation of the decree, see *SEG* 31 (1981) no. 107 and *SEG* 33 (1983) no. 136. See also: Oliver (1941) 133 and Oliver (1972) 190–97, who dates it to 27/26 BC; Day (1942) 146–49, who dates it to the Augustan period; Culley (1975) 207–23 (217 n. 18 lists various scholars and their opinions regarding the date) and Culley (1977) 282–98, who dates it to ca. 10/9–3/2 BC; von Freeden (1983) 174, who dates it to 74/3–65/4 BC; Baldassari (1998) 242–46, also places it in the immediate decades after the attack by Sulla, i.e., the late 70s-50s BC. The most recent and thorough re-analysis concludes that the decree is mid-Augustan in date; see Schmalz (2008) passim; Schmalz (2009) 10–11, 281–82.

6. Robinson (1943) 298; Kienast (2014) 133–35.

private control and was to be restored and/or refurbished by the Romans. There is no indication of what purpose the Tower had served when leased out or what repairs were subsequently to be made.

By the end of Late Antiquity, the Octagon had been adapted for Christian use, as is evidenced by crosses carved into the exterior and interior surfaces and remains of Byzantine paintings on the interior walls. Subsequent to the Ottoman conquest of Athens in the fifteenth century, Muslim scholars utilized the building or the open area near the façade as a meeting place, although the Tower continued to be used by the local Christian community. Toward the middle of the eighteenth century the structure became the property of the Mevlevi sect of Sufi Islam, who converted it into a dervish lodge.

Until the first excavation, by James Stuart and Nicholas Revett (members of the London-based Society of Dilettanti), who resided in Athens from 1751 to 1753, documentation of the monument in the post-classical period for the most part consisted of brief comments by non-Greek travelers who visited Athens between the fifteenth and eighteenth centuries. Stuart and Revett's publication, *The Antiquities of Athens and Other Monuments of Greece,* presented for its time a comprehensive and detailed description of the building.

Over the past seventy years, the Tower of the Winds has been the subject of two monographs and a number of journal articles. In these the Hellenistic architecture, renovations carried out by the Romans, hypotheses regarding the type of interior mechanism, and the date of construction have been comprehensively studied (albeit resulting in widely differing opinions). Other facets and time periods of the building as an operational structure have not been afforded such thorough treatment. Thus, this well-preserved monument from ancient Athens poses a number of questions that remain to be more fully explored.

In this volume, analysis of the Tower's functions throughout its two thousand years of use is presented, reflecting five periods of occupation: Hellenistic (ca. 140–87 BC), post-Sullan Athens (first century BC), Roman (first through sixth centuries AD), Christian (early seventh century through the second quarter of the eighteenth century), and Muslim (ca. 1740–1821). Focusing on the monument's evolving functions and the renovations required by those functions supplies a foundation for the construction of a relative chronology; an absolute chronology is proposed for the time periods when the various alterations and additions to the structure were carried out. This has required reconsideration of all aspects of the edifice, from its original Hellenistic form through its subsequent phases.

Among the conclusions supported by the evidence is a construction date ca. 140 BC, leading to the proposal that the patron can possibly be identified as Attalos II of Pergamon. Because the Tower exhibits architectural features that can be found in Greek monuments identified as cultic or commemorative, the building's function in the Greek and Roman periods can be seen to extend beyond that of a civic structure furnished with meteorological and chronometric instruments in that it also included a religious component designed to honor Boreas and the other wind gods. For the decades after the siege of Athens by Sulla in the early first century BC, when the Octagon was leased to a private individual, the possibility that the water-run mechanism had been looted by the Romans is considered. This would have left an empty, windowless chamber that may have served as a storehouse.

Investigation into the possible types of buildings that served Christian rituals—churches, baptisteries, and martyria—supports the conclusion that the Tower was converted into a martyrium. Identification of the relics that were interred within the monument cannot be established with certainty, but a mid-seventeenth-century reference to the saint as Philip the Greek leads to an examination of whether they may have belonged to the Apostle Philip. The Christian cult remained in place until the eighteenth century, when the Mevlevi sect of whirling dervishes took ownership of the Octagon. At that time, it will be suggested, Philip's cult was moved to the basilica consecrated in his name situated on a site north of the Greek Agora, where tradition says that the apostle preached when he lived in Athens.

This was the last phase in the operational life of the monument. The Greek War of Independence, waged between 1821 and 1832, brought Ottoman rule over Athens to an end. After two millennia of continual use, the Tower of the Winds ceased to be a functional building and became instead an archaeological site.[7]

7. Extensive conservation on the monument was carried out by the Ephorate of Antiquities in Athens in 2014 and 2015. A report on this work, accompanied by numerous photographs, can be found online at: http://efaathculture.gr/wp/content/uploads/2016/05

I

THE HELLENISTIC AND ROMAN TOWER

The Hellenistic Horologion: Overview of the Architecture

The Site

The north-facing Tower of the Winds stands in the area east of the Greek Agora, at the foot of the north slope of the Acropolis almost in line with the Erechtheum above (Frontispiece and Ill. 1). Nearby are a small number of Ottoman buildings surrounded by modern Athens.

The neighborhood of the Horologion in the Hellenistic period cannot be re-created with any degree of certainty. At that time, the monument probably stood in a region that included certain important earlier edifices, although there is much yet to be clarified about the buildings erected there over the centuries.[1] The fact that the ancient ground level around the Tower was approximately seven meters higher than the Greek Agora[2] was perhaps one of the most important features in choosing this location, along with the availability of sufficient space for the building, for the higher elevation would have facilitated the function of its weather vane.

The main road leading to the area of the Octagon branched off the Panathenaic Way (the major thoroughfare in the Greek Agora) and continued unimpeded toward the east, passing along the south side of the monument. The area to the west of the Tower (the site on which the later Roman Agora stood) may have functioned as a marketplace during this period. The expanse immediately in front of the Tower's two porches appears to have been an open plaza, estimated to have been perhaps one hundred by fifty meters. To the southeast of the Horologion (along the north side of the road) stood a large stoa. What structures stood on the east side of the plaza remains unknown.[3]

The extant remains of ancient structures in the immediate vicinity date primarily to the Roman period (Ill. 1). These include, to the west and northwest of the Horologion, the great Roman Agora (whose court was approximately three meters lower than

1. Miller (1995) passim, esp. p. 233, n. 58; Kienast (2014) 23–26.
2. Travlos (1971) 31, 508.
3. Travlos (1971) 281; Hoff (1994) 93–99, 116; Kienast (2014) 21–32, figs. 29, 30, 32, 34.

the Tower), the so-called Library of Hadrian, and a Roman latrine. To the east and southeast at approximately four meters higher than the Tower were two long rectangular buildings: (a) the Hellenistic stoa (mentioned above), which in the Roman period was enclosed with an entrance provided in its now solid western end wall, and (b) to its south a two-story stoa (as currently reconstructed) dating to the mid-first century AD that is commonly referred to erroneously as the Agoranomion (the offices of the market officials). These two buildings were separated by a long rectangular courtyard whose entrance consisted of an arcuated wall, the foundation for which lies atop the *crepidoma* of the Tower's annex (Ills. 6a-c).[4] Along with providing access to the courtyard of the "Agoranomion", the arched entrance wall supported an aqueduct that carried water to the Horologion, thus replacing an underground water channel from the Hellenistic period that apparently no longer functioned due to extensive construction in the area. The east-west road leading from the Panathenaic Way now culminated at the west entrance of the Roman Agora. Across from the east entrance of the market, in order to accommodate the significant increase in ground level, a flight of stairs led up to the arcuated wall.[5]

The Exterior of the Building

The Tower of the Winds is a single-story octagonal edifice of Pentelic marble on a three-stepped *crepidoma* with a semicircular annex projecting from the rear (south) wall. The structure measures eight meters in diameter (3.26 meters per octagonal side) and 13.85 meters in height.[6] It is accurately oriented on a north-south axis, deviating a mere 0.016 meters off due north.

The building had two distyle prostyle pedimented porches on the northeast and northwest walls (Ills. 2–5). Five fragments of a Corinthian entablature, recovered from excavation debris near the northwest porch, consist of a triple-fascia architrave, an unadorned frieze course, dentils, and four lion-head water spouts on the lateral simas; central and side acroteria (not extant) adorned the pediment (Ills. 7a, 7b).[7] The lower portions of monolithic column shafts from the northwest porch were found in situ; a third partial column lay on the ground nearby. The porches were of a mixed order. The column shafts have 20 flutes and stand directly on the pavement with no base, as in the Doric order, combined with Ionic fillets (Ill. 8a).

Unfortunately, the capitals are missing, and differing opinions have been offered as to their form. Stuart and Revett suggest that an acanthus-lotus capital found in their

4. Korres (1996) 144, fig. 8; Kienast (2014) figs. 34 and 35.
5. For a synopsis of research on buildings in this area and pertinent bibliography, see Greco (2014) 759–61, figs. 422–424, 426 ("Agoranomion"); 762–65, figs. 425–427 (Hellenistic stoa); 770–776, figs. 434–438 (Roman Agora); 780–87, figs. 441–450 ("Library of Hadrian").
6. Kienast (2014) 42, 106.
7. Stuart and Revett (1762) Ch. 3, pp. 14, 19, pl. 7; Stuart and Revett (1825), Ch. 3, p. 45, pls. 14, 16; von Freeden (1983) 79–85, pls. 13–15; Kienast (1997) 56; Kienast (2014) 79–83; figs. 120–122.

excavations may belong to one of the Tower's porches, although they moderate their statement by saying that it "did perhaps never belong to it. . . . This example of capital was profusely used at Athens." They conclude that it more likely dates to the period after the "Roman conquest."[8] Coulton supports Stuart and Revett's original restoration of the porches with the acanthus-lotus capital. He believes that the order of the Horologion was influenced by Pergamene architecture in that the precursor of this type of capital is to be found on that city's propylon of the Sanctuary of Demeter, which was built in the first half of the second century BC under the patronage of Apollonis, the mother of Eumenes II and Attalos II.[9] Coulton does not note, however, that the composition of the acanthus-lotus capital found by Stuart and Revett is different from the capitals in the Demeter Sanctuary, which has lotus leaves with no acanthus. Also, the column shafts from the Pergamene propylon, unlike those from the Horologion, are completely Doric in that they stand directly on the pavement with no base and, although unfinished, are carved on the lowest several centimeters with 20 Doric flutes.[10]

Von Freeden suggests that the capitals were Doric because the columns have no bases, and he believes that the Tower's engaged interior colonnade—which consists of columns with no bases, Ionic fillets, and Doric capitals—reflects the structure of the porch.[11] Kienast believes that the capitals were Corinthian and thus would coordinate with other elements from the exterior: (a) the acanthus finial on the Octagon roof, (b) the Corinthian entablatures of the porches, and (c) the column shafts, which follow the rules for Corinthian capitals.[12] The evidence does not lead to a clear conclusion, however, and arguments can be made in support of the proposals by both von Freeden and Kienast.

Bi-leaf doors (which opened inward) were framed by simple linear moldings with Doric "ears" at the top. The entrances are 3.55 meters high, measuring 2.10 meters wide at the top and 2.25 meters at the bottom (Ill. 9).[13]

No remains of a dedicatory inscription are extant. The entablature of the northwest porch clearly demonstrates that there was none on the north side of the building. Kienast suggests that one may have been inscribed on blocks (now missing) from the upper course of the semicircular annex on the south side. He admits that this would have been an unusual location for a dedication but states that it would have made the inscription visible to passersby walking along the main east-west street in the area, which lay approximately four meters to the south of the Tower. This hypothesis has led Kienast to regard the south side as the main façade of the Octagon, with the porches on the rear.[14] It is difficult to accept, however, that Athenian observers would view the

8. Stuart and Revett (1762) 14, pl. 6.3; Stuart and Revett (1825) 43–44 and n. a, pl. 16.1.
9. Coulton (1976) 123, figs. 31.f and g, pl. 14.
10. Bohtz (1981) 17–20, pls. 10, 12, 45.
11. Von Freeden (1983) 82–83, pl. 22.2.
12. Kienast (1997) 56; Kienast (2014) 78–83.
13. Kienast (2014) 76–79, fig. 117, pls. 9 and 34a.
14. Kienast (2014) 27, 135.

wall on the opposite side of the building from the entrance doors as the main façade, even taking a dedicatory inscription into consideration.

The Pentelic marble is of very high quality. The surface was worked with a toothed chisel in a manner that heightened the reflectivity of the crystals in the stone. The exterior walls of the Tower are demarcated into four zones over fifteen courses that mirror the articulated divisions of the interior walls. The three lower zones are separated by narrow headers, which are the exterior faces of interior ornamental cornices. Eight sundials (the bronze gnomons are missing) are engraved on the exterior of Zone 3 and are the only accurate vertical sundials extant from the classical period.[15] An arched niche carved into the exterior west wall of Zone 3 can be dated to the post-classical period, since it was cut into one of the hour lines of a sundial (Ill. 11). It is difficult to conclude with certainty, however, what purpose it may have served in the monument's later phases. The niche is similar in shape to religious shrines found in Orthodox Christianity. In Late Antique and medieval Athens the niche would have been quite high above ground level, but it is possible that it could have contained an icon. An alternative option regarding its function is suggested by its orientation, which puts the niche nearly on axis with a mihrab installed inside the building in the eighteenth century when the Tower was under Muslim ownership. The size, shape, and flat rear wall of the niche recall exterior Islamic shrines (flat mihrabs) that serve for individual devotion.[16] After the assault on Athens by the Venetians in 1687, which resulted in the destruction of the Parthenon and left the streets piled high with debris, the niche would have been significantly closer to a worshipper, for by then the ground level was approximately five meters above the Tower's foundations. An illustration made by James Stuart a century later (published in 1762) shows adjacent buildings and walls very close to or up against the Octagon, rendering access to the niche by that time seemingly somewhat problematic (Ill. 40).

Windows in the top course of the north and west walls in Zone 3 also are not original, as the west window obliterates part of one sundial, and the north window is in the middle of another (Frontispiece; Ills. 5, 11). Consequently, they date to some point after the bronze gnomons had been removed, when the sundials would no longer have been functional. Evidence for the windows having been made in the eighteenth century at the time the building was converted for Muslim use by the Mevlevi dervishes is provided by illustrations depicting the exterior and interior of the Octagon. A sketch by Richard Pococke made in 1735 displays no windows, while another by Richard Dalton from 1749 shows both windows, although he erroneously depicts the west window on the southwest wall (Ills. 38, 39).[17] The removal of the block from the west wall illuminates the east interior wall near the mihrab (Ills. 11, 15). Light coming through the opening on the north side illuminates the lower portion of the south wall of the main chamber.

15. Gibbs (1976) 42–45; Kienast (2014) 91–92.
16. For flat mihrabs, see Dickie (1978) 33–34.
17. Pococke (1745) pl. 76; Dalton (1791) fig. 53.

Zone 4 on the exterior of the Tower consists of eight personifications of wind gods sculptured in high relief, posed horizontally flying toward the right (Ills. 2, 3, 20, 21). Behind the head and wings of each figure are two fasciae bordered above by a projecting molding (a narrow fillet and an ovolo). Across the top is a tall recessed band with a narrow aperture (ca. 0.03 meters long and 0.05 meters high) at its center, which provides weak illumination to the top course of the interior walls and the ceiling. The name of the god is inscribed at the left of the aperture. The fact that they are centrally placed with the deities' names inscribed at the left is evidence that these openings are part of the original construction.

The roof is composed of marble pan-and-cover tiles laid in eight triangular sections; an octagonal sima supports three lion's head water spouts per side.[18] At the apex is a fragmentary marble finial consisting—in its damaged condition—of a *kalathos* adorned with two rows of acanthus leaves, which Stuart and Revett found lying on the lower part of the Tower's roof.[19] Although the Dilettanti describe it as having thin "palm" (i.e., lotus) leaves behind the acanthus, the finial contains only acanthus leaves. Instead of the usual four volutes there are eight, thus reflecting the octagonal form of the monument. Atop the finial, according to Vitruvius, was a bronze weather vane in the form of a Triton. This is the earliest verifiable permanent construction of a weather vane.[20] In his right hand was a wand that would point in the direction from which the wind was currently blowing, thus toward the sculptured figure of the appropriate wind god.

Robinson and von Freeden assert that Varro describes an interior weather vane in the Horologion that would have allowed someone to know the wind direction even when standing within the Athenian building.[21] This is an apparent misreading of the passage in *De Re Rustica.* There Varro is referring to an internal indicator in his rotunda in Casinum, not in the Horologion in Athens. Varro's point of comparison between the two buildings is not in regard to internal weather vanes but instead is to the fact that both had depictions of eight wind gods.

The Annex

Attached to the south side of the building is a semicircular annex.[22] Four courses are fully preserved, and another three remain in part (Ills. 10a, 10b). The structure measures

18. Terracotta tiles covering the joins of the marble roof tiles are modern and were installed in 1919 to control leakage.
19. Stuart and Revett (1762) 19; Stuart and Revett (1825) 43–44, pl. 15.5; von Freeden (1983) pl. 7.1; Kienast (1997) 64 n. 35; Kienast (2014) 62–64, figs. 94 and 95b.
20. The first wind indicators likely consisted of strips of cloth attached to trees or poles. A passage from the "Fable of the Willow", however, may indicate permanent weather vanes existed in Mesopotamia in the Akkadian period: "Like a headband, the temple is adorned with [. . .]. They look at the [b]ird of the wind to test the wind;" see Horowitz (1998) 198.
21. Robinson (1943) 293; von Freeden (1983) 2–3.
22. Kienast (1997) 59 and fig. 6 (the orientation of the building is accurately described in the text, but the diagram is incorrect in that the directional arrow points south instead of north); Kienast (2014) 40, 83–90, figs. 45 and 127–132, pl. 39.

2.96 meters in diameter and projects 2.30 meters from the south wall of the Tower. On its east and west sides are vertical ventilation/illumination slots ca. 0.50 meters wide and 0.80 meters high. Engraved on its curved surface is a ninth sundial. On the basis of drawings by Stuart and Revett, as cited by Kienast, the now missing annex roof was pyramidal, with dentils and moldings similar to those that adorned the porches.[23]

The interior of the annex is divided into upper and lower sections by a stone shelf.[24] This small platform supported a water tank, the bottom of which was at the same level as the lowest interior cornice in the main chamber, approximately two meters above floor level, a height that would have allowed for the requisite water pressure for the functioning of a complex mechanical device. A narrow crawl space along one side creates an opening between the two sections of the annex. In the center of the floor is a slightly irregular square hole (ca. 0.40 meters by 0.50 meters) that penetrates three courses of the foundation to a channel that runs beneath the building. A second aperture (a small circular hole) abuts the south wall in which, directly above, is carved a vertical channel for a water pipe. The channel is wider at the bottom than at the top, indicating this was an inflow water pipe that would have fed into the collecting tank. Unfortunately, investigating how water was delivered into the annex through this pipe has not been carried out, for it would require excavation that would cause damage to the foundation of the monument. Once inside, water flowed from the annex to the octagonal chamber through an underground pipe, with no direct access between the main room and the annex. When rare (one assumes) repairs were needed, it is thought that outside the building was an entrance to a maintenance shaft that led into the underground channel. This would have permitted a slender person—with some difficulty—to crawl through the drain in the floor, thus providing access to the lower and upper levels of the annex.[25]

The Interior of the Main Chamber

The diameter of the octagonal main chamber of the Tower is 7.96 meters when measured from angle to angle and 6.85 meters when measured from the centers of opposing walls. The room is 10.50 meters high from the floor to the rim of the domed ceiling and 12.50 meters to the keystone. The interior walls are divided into four zones that, as mentioned above, correspond to the exterior wall divisions (Ills. 4, 12, 17a, 17b).

Zone 1 consists of two ashlar courses and an unadorned cornice composed of a tall fillet surmounted by two narrower projecting fillets (Ill. 13).

Zone 2 consists of four ashlar courses. Its cornice has dentils and three fasciae supported by curved consoles with a single groove on the underside (Ill. 14a, 14b). Carved

23. Kienast (2014) 86–88, fig. 130.
24. Kienast (2014) pl. 40.
25. Kienast (2014) 146.

into the southeast angle of the walls (immediately above the first cornice) is a mihrab, which was created by the Muslim dervishes (Ill. 15).[26]

Zone 3, which carries the sundials on the exterior, consists of four ashlar courses that protrude approximately 0.05 meters beyond the lower walls. The face of the third cornice is not octagonal but is a smooth circular band, ca. 0.33 meters deep, formed by inserting shallow triangular blocks in the angles of the eight wall joins (Ill. 16).

Zone 4 consists of two ashlar courses. On the lower course (whose exterior contains the bodies of the wind gods) are eight engaged mixed-order columns (1.12 and 1.13 meters tall), standing on lead plates, at each of the Octagon's wall joins (Ills. 16, 17a, 17b).[27] The monolithic columns consist of twenty flutes on shafts with no base and Doric capitals with three necking rings. The upper two-thirds of the shafts are fluted with Ionic fillets, while the vertical segments on the lower third are filled in. Above is a plain architrave and an unsculptured frieze course beneath a projecting molding, reflecting components on the exterior face of the building. An area of the frieze course on the southeast preserves remains of a painted anthemion. Small amounts of paint have also been identified on the ceiling. With pigment extant on six of the ceiling slabs (nos. 3, 6, 9, 12, 16, and 18), it is clear that the entire surface was painted in a glittering Egyptian blue denoting a night sky. Indentations in the marble indicate that the dome was also adorned with figures of some sort.[28] Stars were likely to have been part of the decoration. An account written by Evliya Çelebi, a Turkish visitor to Athens in 1668, describes the ceiling as being adorned with images of astronomical bodies.[29]

Almost all light entering the building was provided by the two entrance doors when opened. There were other more subtle sources of light created by the architect, however. First, the marble surfaces on the interior walls were finished in two different techniques. The lower two zones were worked with a toothed chisel in the same manner as the exterior but to an even smoother texture. The upper two zones were worked with a pointed chisel, resulting in a surface that is coarser and more granular than the exterior walls. Both methods were intended to maximize the reflection of the light that entered through the two doors. Second, the wall blocks at the eight angles of Zone 4 do not join; they are separated by a gap ca. 0.03 meters wide that allows light to enter the area behind each miniature column. Third, as mentioned above, narrow slits penetrate the

26. Robinson (1943) 291 n. 1, mistakenly identifies the mihrab as part of the Christian renovations: "An apsidal niche, cut into the southeast wall on the interior, between the first and second cornices, testifies to the use of the building as a Christian chapel." Inwood (1827) 122–23, pl. 19, with no evidentiary foundation, suggests a sculptured frieze with figures resembling the exterior reliefs may have been placed above the first cornice. His hypothesis included a freestanding figure that would have been controlled by a water clock and which would have turned to point at various figures in the relief.

27. Stuart and Revett (1762) pl. 9.4; Stuart and Revett (1825) pls. 18.2, 18.4; von Freeden (1983) pls. 20.1, 21.2, 22.1, 23.1; Kienast (2014) 54, fig. 79, pl. 29b.

28. Kienast (2014) 94–96 and nn. 294 and 295, figs. 138–140.

29. Dankoff and Kim (2010) 289. "Çelebi" is an Ottoman title that is the equivalent of Gentleman or Esquire.

marble above the wind god reliefs. On the interior, the faces of these slits are significantly enlarged and are fashioned in a manner that creates a strong upward angle, thus directing light toward the ceiling. Despite their size, these apertures would have been obscured by the projecting architrave above the miniature columns, making them invisible to the viewer below. Both sets of openings in Zone 4 allowed diffuse light to penetrate at this level, supplying indirect illumination to the colonnade and the decorated dome.[30]

Evidence for how the building may have functioned on the interior is indicated by the architectural elements, by cuttings made into the marble surfaces of the floors and walls, and by the condition of those surfaces. Unfortunately, dispositive answers are not easily ascertained, and a number of conclusions remain in the realm of the hypothetical.

Examination of the lower interior walls and the floors produces a very short list of architectural features that can be attributed with absolute confidence to the original Hellenistic structure. These include, as described above, the elements in the annex: the vertical pipe channel in the south wall above the small intake hole in the floor and the square drain in the center of the annex floor, which connected to the underground channel. In the main chamber of the Tower, they consist of a hole in the center of the floor (referred to in most publications as the "central drain") and three circular indentations that were bedding for freestanding columns (Ill. 5).

The large round central aperture (ca. 0.50 meters in diameter) within the oblong central floor block of the main chamber penetrates the foundation to the ground beneath and connects to the underground channel that lies on a north-south axis under the building.[31] The hole, which is slightly lower than floor level, is encircled by a flat border into which seven radial grooves were carved. One groove is obliterated by a channel for a water pipe added later by the Romans (Ills. 18, 32). Each of the grooves ends in a small circular depression at the outer edge. Water under pressure traveled underground through a pipe from the annex and emerged from this aperture to power a hydraulic mechanism. Kienast thinks that the grooves in the border of the aperture are original to the Hellenistic monument and may have anchored the support for this device. He does find it odd that there are only seven grooves, given that the architect expressed the number eight elsewhere throughout his architectural plan. Having only seven grooves instead of eight is, however, suggestive of this being a later refinement, and the possibility should be entertained that at some point in the history of the Tower when the water-run mechanism was no longer in situ and water had ceased to flow, the grooves may have been added to anchor a protective grill cover.

The three column beddings lie in an arc on the south side of the chamber—on NE-SW, N-S, and NW-SE axes—1.10 meters from the central aperture. They measure approximately 0.45 meters in diameter and 0.10 meters deep. As expression of the precision

30. Kienast (2014) 69, 93–94, 96, figs. 99–101.

31. Stuart and Revett (1762) 15; Stuart and Revett (1825) 40; Noble and Price (1968) 346–47; Kienast (1997) 58 and nn. 20 and 21; Kienast (2014) 37–38, figs. 49–51; pl. 38.

one finds throughout the Hellenistic plan, the middle cavity is exactly on the north-south axis, in line with the central aperture and the midline of the elongated central floor block into which it is carved. The two flanking cavities lie a meter to either side, the outer edge of each abutting the outer edge of the trapezoidal floor block. These beddings obviously held freestanding columns of approximately the same diameter (height unknown) as those in the two porches. That the columns were part of the original Hellenistic construction is demonstrated by the fact they do not overlie other nearby cuttings in the floor—curved bedding grooves for segments of a balustrade (which I propose was part of Christian renovations) and straight channels for water pipes (part of the Roman renovations). Those cuttings do, however, make accommodation for the three circular cavities in that the channels and curved grooves are angled around or shortened to abut the column footings. Noble and Price suggested that the columns both supported elements of a water clock and acted as supports for statues. Kienast rejects their hypotheses and leaves the question open.[32] They certainly must, however, have been an integral part of a very sophisticated visual and scientific display.

The floors reveal varied patterns of use. The northeast threshold exhibits a great deal of wear, while the northwest threshold exhibits almost none (Ills. 8a, 8b, 8c). Thus, access to the building seems to have been via the northeast door to a far greater extent—or almost exclusively—over one or more periods of occupation. The floor of the main chamber shows wear from having been walked on by many people over many years and also from erosion due to water damage; the floor of the annex shows no wear.[33] The following discussion regarding various cuttings in the floor derives from these observations.

Two series of small holes in the floor of the main chamber seem not to be part of the original construction but were installed, I suggest, at some point before the Roman renovations in the first century AD. The first series has eight small shallow, somewhat irregular, nearly round holes (ca. 0.06 meters in diameter and 0.05 meters deep), that lie immediately outside the bedding grooves for the balustrade and delineate a circular area approximately 3.50 meters in diameter (1.50 meters from the walls) at the center of the chamber. Fifteen small holes of the same size and workmanship encircle the perimeter of the room except for the area immediately in front of the northeast door (Ill. 19). Their placement follows a pattern within each of the trapezoidal floor blocks—three holes at the outer edge along the wall and two at the inner border (near the balustrade grooves), which creates the outline of an outer and inner octagon (Ill. 33). Because they are identical, the two series of holes can be considered to be contemporary. Several hypotheses have been proposed to explain their connection to the building's access and what function they performed.

Robinson, who ascribes them to the original Hellenistic design, argues that the lack of a hole in front of the northeast door with its more worn threshold indicates this was

32. Price (1967) 586–96; Noble and Price (1968) 353, pls. 118.18 and 19; Kienast (2014) 38–39.
33. Kienast (2014) 37.

the sole public access to the building from the very beginning, while the northwest door was always closed and locked.[34] He suggests that the holes may have anchored bronze foot rails or waist-high fences of posts and chains.

Noble and Price argue that the two series of holes might have accommodated pins for anchoring a removable wood floor, surmising it would have protected visitors' feet from surplus water spilling from the annex. They note that when walking into the building one has to step quite far down from the entrance to the level of the marble floor; thus, there is ample space to accommodate raised flooring.[35] In the end, they conclude, it is more likely that the wood floor was part of Christian renovations. Noble and Price's conclusions are problematic, however. First, they offer no suggestions as to under what conditions or how often the floor would have been installed and over what period of time it would have been employed. Second, they do not comment on the fact that the surface of the marble floor in the main chamber shows significant erosion not just from water but also from having been walked on extensively. Third, if Christian architects altered or made repairs to the marble pavement, I think it likely that they would have laid a new marble floor or a mosaic floor, not one of wood.

Kienast, while concurring with Robinson that one door would have been sufficient for access, does not believe that the northwest door was always or primarily kept closed because this would have impeded the movement of air and significantly reduced the amount of light. Because he finds the workmanship of the two series of small holes to be somewhat irregular, he considers them to be incompatible with the design standards of the Tower; thus, he thinks they must not have been part of the original construction. As for their function, he agrees with Noble and Price that the holes probably were created at some point to anchor a wood floor. Kienast states that the specific purpose for such an addition remains obscure, but he believes it somehow worked in relation to the water-run mechanism.[36]

Small, who proposes that the Tower was converted to a baptistery during Late Antiquity, thinks the two sets of small holes in the floor were designed to anchor slender wood or stone columns that enclosed a baptismal font and articulated the walls. He reconstructs the eight columns surrounding the *fons vitae* with a canopy (*tegurium*) similar in form to that in the early fifth-century Lateran Baptistery in Rome and suggests its weight would have helped keep the columns in place. He also proposes that a second higher canopy may have rested on the outer ring of columns.[37] Small's hypothesis has not been generally accepted.

34. Robinson (1943) 296, fig. 4.

35. Noble and Price (1968) 348. The authors believed the access door between the main chamber and the annex was an original component of the building.

36. Kienast (2014) 41–42.

37. Small (1980) passim. When Stuart and Revett removed approximately 2,700 cubic meters of soil, stones, and other debris from the interior, in which they found sections of the marble balustrade, they did not report finding any remains of a *tegurium* or encircling colonnade. See Stuart and Revett (1762) 14; Stuart and Revett (1825) 37–38.

Regarding the relationship between the small holes and the doors of the Octagon, I find it not just highly unlikely but completely untenable to think that the building would have been designed with two entrances near one another on the same side if only one was to be opened on a regular basis. If a single door was considered adequate for the presupposed number of visitors, then a porch on the north side directly beneath the personification of Boreas would have served the purpose and, architecturally, would have been balanced by the annex on the opposite side of the building. Kienast's point regarding both doors being needed to supply adequate light and air certainly makes sense.

As for the purpose of the holes, I think Robinson arrives at the most probable answer when he suggests that they would have anchored bronze posts (of undetermined height) from which chains would have been suspended. A post-and-chain barrier around the perimeter might have performed two functions. The hole in front of the northwest threshold indicates that at some point after the Octagon was inaugurated and opened to the public, the decision was made to funnel access solely through the northeast door while keeping both doors opened to allow for maximum light and airflow. The perimeter barrier might also have served as protection for objects displayed along the walls beneath the first cornice. Among various possibilities, for example, Price suggests that star calendars (*parapegmata*), which recorded the risings and settings of major stars and constellations throughout the year, may have been exhibited.[38] Post-and-chain fencing encircling the central area of the room would have served as protection from visitors for the mechanical device yet allowed an attendant admittance (one could unlatch the chain).

It has generally been assumed by scholars who have investigated this monument that protection for the mechanism was provided by the balustrade, which has been considered to be part of the original Hellenistic construction. Viewing the balustrade's date and function in this manner has precluded consideration of the possibility that the small holes instead performed this function in the Hellenistic building. It should be noted that the curved grooves for the balustrade are more crudely worked than the small holes and that their placement lacks coordination with regard to the octagonal plan of the monument. These two points lead me to believe that the balustrade was added at a later period, and I will argue below it belongs to the Christian renovations. The somewhat irregular workmanship of the small holes, as Kienast points out, *is* contradictory to the standards of the Hellenistic architect. Their pattern of placement in the floor, however, demonstrates an effort was made to incorporate them into the octagonal formula of the architectural plan. This combination of imperfect workmanship and considered placement would seem to be an indication that the small holes are not part of the original Hellenistic construction but instead precede the Roman

38. Price (1964) 14. There are no holes in the surfaces of the lower walls or in the first cornice to indicate that objects were suspended. Thus, anything displayed would have to have been freestanding. For discussion of *parapegma*, see Evans (1999) 256–59, fig. 16.

renovations, which were carried out without consideration for the exactitude evidenced in the Octagon's Hellenistic design.

In conclusion, the solution I propose here for incorporating these factors into the layout and function of the Tower is, admittedly, hypothetical. I suggest that when the Hellenistic monument was opened to visitors both doors were in use, and there was no barrier around the mechanism. At some point—perhaps not very long afterward—the changes discussed above were found to be necessary. A post-and-chain barrier was placed around the device, a similar arrangement encircled the perimeter of the chamber (perhaps to protect some sort of visual display), and traffic (for some undetermined reason) was directed primarily through the northeast door while allowing access to maximum light and air by having both doors open.

The Relief Sculpture

The sculptured frieze depicting personifications of the winds contains eight winged male figures posed horizontally toward the right as though in flight (Ills. 20, 21). Each is located on the side of the building facing the direction from which the wind originates. On the front of the monument over the northeast and northwest porches are personifications of Kaikias and Skiron. Between them in the most prominent position is Boreas. The remaining personifications, from east to west, are Apeliotes, Euros, Notos, Lips, and Zephyros.[39] Four of the figures are mature bearded males (northwest, north, northeast, and south), and four are youthful and beardless (east, west, south, and southwest). The name of each figure is carved into the left side of the molding directly above. Included with seven of the personifications are attributes indicating the season and type of weather during which they are most active. The relief figures on the Horologion are the earliest surviving visual representations of the Greek wind gods. It is not known whether their attributes are the invention of the architect and sculptor or whether they derive from some other source.

Descriptions

1. *Boreas.* The north wind brings cold, turbulent storms. The figure, in very good condition, is a physically powerful mature male with a heavy beard and long unruly hair. His face is in three-quarter view toward the right. He wears a long-sleeved knee-length garment (probably of wool) with a narrow belt across the chest over the overfold.

39. Total length = 26 meters. Relief figures = ca. 2.50 m long and 1.70 m high. Stuart and Revett (1825) 47–49, pl. 21; von Freeden (1983) pls. 3, 8, 9, 24–42; Simon, *LIMC,* 8 (1997), *s.v.* "Venti", no. 12; Kienast (2014) 169, pls. 19, 21–25. Jacques Carrey drew four of the figures (Boreas, Kaikias, Notos, Apeliotes) in 1674 when he was copying the Parthenon sculptures; see Omont (1898) 6, pl. 21. They are, however, rough sketches compared to the detailed representations of Stuart and Revett.

One end of a medium-length mantle flutters across the right shoulder; the other end—full of wind like a sail—is gripped in his left hand. Tassels adorn the visible corners of the mantle. The god is shod in *embades* (closed calf-high boots) and *piloi* (socks) with jagged edges hanging down, which are held in place over the boot top with a garter. Poised gently on the outstretched right hand is a conch shell, a reference to the sound of the north wind as it roared down mountains, through city streets, or across the waves.

2. *Kaikias.* The northeast wind brings cold, damp, cloudy weather, including rain, snow, and hailstorms. This heavily muscled figure, similar to Boreas, is in fair condition. The partially eroded head displays a frontal face, long unruly hair, and a long, full beard. He wears a sleeveless tunic, unpinned at the right shoulder, with overfold; the heavy fabric billows above the knees. A medium-length mantle wraps around both upper arms. Like Boreas, he wears *embades* and *piloi* with garters. Kaikias holds a round metal shield, inside facing out, the lower half of which is filled with small pebbles—suggesting the sound made by a hailstorm.

3. *Apeliotes.* The east wind brings the gentle, steady rain needed for plant life. The figure's head and feet are damaged; the face, in three-quarter view toward the right, is nearly completely sheared off. The god is a young, beardless, lithe male. He wears a knee-length sleeveless tunic unpinned at the right shoulder. His mantle, with tassels at the corners, is draped over the left shoulder, with the other end wrapped around his upper right arm. He wears *embades* and *piloi* like those described above. The swag of the mantle is filled with samples of nature's bounty—fruit, vegetables, and honeycomb.

4. *Euros.* The southeast wind brings dark, rainy, humid weather. The figure is a mature, muscular, bearded male with medium-length hair, the neatly arranged strands blowing back from his face. His head, in profile toward the right, is damaged in the area of the nose. He wears a sleeveless tunic unpinned at the right shoulder. His long mantle, with tassels on the corners, billows above the left shoulder and is gripped in his left hand, while the other end entirely encloses the right arm and hand, leaving the right shoulder and upper chest exposed. He is shod in *embades* and jagged-edged *piloi.* He carries no separate attribute.

5. *Notos.* The south wind, Boreas' brother, brings hot and humid weather. He is a youthful male with long, neat hair. His face, which has suffered significant damage, looks downward in three-quarter profile toward the right. He wears a knee-length sleeveless tunic, unpinned at the right shoulder, and a mantle with tassels at the corners draped over the left shoulder. He is shod with *embades* and jagged-edged *piloi.* A water jar (badly damaged) is cradled upside down in the right arm, connoting the rains of late summer.

6. *Lips.* The southwest wind was able to blow ships directly into the port of Piraeus or make it difficult for them to depart. He is a youthful, beardless male. The face, which is in three-quarter view toward the right (the nose and left side of the mouth are destroyed), and the hairstyle resemble Notos. Lips wears a knee-length sleeveless tunic unpinned at the right shoulder. A mantle with a tassel at the visible corner is draped over his left shoulder and then wraps or is rolled around the waist, leaving the right arm

and upper chest uncovered. He is barefoot. With both hands he holds a four-pronged *aphlaston,* the ornamented curved element from the stern of a ship.

7. *Zephyros.* The west wind, brother of Boreas and Notos, brings warm weather in the spring but is hot and humid in summer. He is a youthful beardless male with neat medium-length hair. The figure has suffered severe damage to the frontally posed face, which at some point has been re-created in concrete. The lower legs and feet are heavily damaged. The lithe body is nude except for a long mantle that wraps across the back and billows out beneath the right arm. He is barefoot. On the left side the drapery creates a swag, supported by both hands, that is filled with flower blossoms.

8. *Skiron.* The northwest wind is very cold in winter and very hot in summer with frequent lightning. Similar to Boreas, Skiron is depicted as a mature male with a full beard and long unruly hair. The figure is in good condition except for damage to the nose and mouth. The head is in three-quarter view toward the right. He is dressed in a knee-length sleeved tunic with a wide, flat belt across the chest over the overfold. He is shod in *embades* and jagged-edged *piloi* held in place by a garter. He holds a large vessel upside down, which Stuart and Revett suggest may be a representation of a bronze firepot, thus a reference to the dryness of the wind and the lightning it creates.[40]

Examination of the sculptural style of the Octagon's relief figures does not in and of itself establish the date of their execution, for by the Hellenistic period craftsmen had acquired the capability to create figures in a variety of styles from various periods; their work is a product of choice rather than the product of a prevailing fashion. A good example of the diverse abilities and choices of Hellenistic sculptors can be found on the Pergamon Altar, where the Baroque carving style of the Gigantomachy frieze from the exterior stands in contrast to the cooler, more classicizing style of the Telephos frieze from the interior. Specific details in the figures of the Horologion, as in other Hellenistic reliefs, however, can serve as chronological indicators.

It is in fact the great Attalid monument in Pergamon (ca. 165–160 BC) that is most frequently evoked in comparison with the sculpture from the Tower where the large powerfully built wind gods have been likened to the admittedly more complexly posed figures in the Gigantomachy frieze (Ills. 22, 23).[41] Such comparisons invariably favor the quality of the sculpture on the Altar over the reliefs on the Horologion, with the Athenian figures described as flat, less animated, and less accomplished.[42] The Altar's sculpture is of such high quality that in truth, most (if not all) other Hellenistic architectural reliefs suffer when they are considered side by side. In regard to the quality of the carving of the Tower's wind gods, I agree with Stuart and Revett, who describe the mood of the reliefs as "noble, bold sculpture, both for design and execution."[43]

40. Stuart and Revett (1825) 49; von Freeden(1983) pls. 27–31.1, 40.3, 41.2, 42.2; Simon, *LIMC* 8 (1997), *s.v.* "Venti", no. 12.369.

41. Callaghan (1981) 115–21; Webb (1996) 61–66; Webb (1998) 244–52; de Luca and Radt (1999) 124–25.

42. Von Freeden (1983) 121–28; Robinson (1984) 424.

43. Stuart and Revett (1762) 14; Stuart and Revett (1825) 38.

Ridgway, while tentatively conceding to those who date the Tower to the first century BC, thinks that the wind reliefs could be taken as nearly contemporary with the Pergamene Gigantomachy. She notes that the figures in the friezes of both monuments are identified by inscriptions bearing their names and points out several other features in common, including unruly hair, deeply set eyes, modeled foreheads, and comparable footwear. She states that the drapery on the wind reliefs shows fifth-century mannerisms that one can find in the Gigantomachy, although "perhaps at a slightly later stage because of the frequent 'trumpet folds' over the figures' thighs." As other indications of a somewhat lower date, Ridgway points out differences in the wing feathers, a "clumsy" rendering of torsion in the figures, and the classicizing style of the youthful faces.[44]

Karanastasi, in a comprehensive examination of the Tower's reliefs, focuses her stylistic analysis primarily on the heads of the bearded wind gods because of their better state of preservation, although she also appraises the costumes and attributes.[45] She presents a number of examples of figures in the round and in relief that she believes demonstrate carving styles similar to the Tower's reliefs. Unfortunately, the various sculptures cannot be confined to a narrow time frame and instead date across a fairly broad chronological range or cannot be reliably dated. Thus, they provide inappreciable clarification of the chronology of the Tower reliefs. Among the examples she presents and the dates she accepts for the sculptures are:[46] (a) a freestanding figure attributed to the roof of the Pergamon Altar and tentatively identified as Poseidon, which she dates later than the Altar but before 138 BC; (b) the Poseidon from Melos, late third to late second centuries BC; (c) four satyrs' masks on a round altar from the Theater of Dionysus in Athens, ca. 120 BC; (d) the head of Zeus from the Heroon of Leon at Kalydon, ca. 100 BC; (e) the Lakrateides Relief, ca. 100 BC, although she considers the wind reliefs to be earlier than this Eleusinian sculpture; and (f) the dead giants from the Small Attalid Dedication on the Athenian Acropolis, ca. 159–138.[47]

Karanastasi's most consistent comparisons, however, are with elements from the friezes on the Pergamon Altar. Like Ridgway, she considers the deeply carved locks and the deeply embedded eyes of the wind gods to be in the tradition of the Gigantomachy, although at a certain distance. Other Pergamene *comparanda* she notes include a giant from the north frieze, poses in the Telephos frieze, and wings in the Gigantomachy (which she states express unambiguous similarities to those of the wind gods).[48] She also concludes that certain details (such as the drapery of Notos and Euros) are noticeably high Baroque in style and certainly have connections with the Attalid monument.

44. Ridgway (2000) 32–42; (2002) 52–54.
45. Karanastasi (2014) 176–93.
46. Karanastasi (2014) 177–81, and nn. 691, 694, 696, 698, 701, 702.
47. The figures from the Small Attalid Dedication are problematic as *comparanda* for they are marble copies of Greek bronze originals that are not extant. Moreover, the date of the monument is in contention. While Stewart (2004) 218–20, among others, attributes it to Attalos I, ca. 200 B.C., some scholars believe it was commissioned by Attalos II in the mid-second century B.C.
48. Karanastasi (2014) 181, 189, and nn. 703, 733, 739.

She also points out that the cosmological and astronomical aspects of the Horologion relate it to the Pergamon Altar. These elements, however, she considers to be either the product of the carvers looking back to an earlier period or traits that continued throughout the second century BC.[49] In the end, Karanastasi concludes that the larger details of the wind reliefs fit Kienast's date for the Octagon of ca. 120–100 BC, thus rejecting the possibility that the date of the Tower and its sculpture may be a few decades earlier and closer in time to the Pergamon Altar.

Lauter also proposes a late second-century date for the Tower as a result of his comparison between the wind gods and figures of Nikai on altars at Kos, which he dates to sometime before 100 BC. He especially notes the disjointed torsion with frontal or nearly frontal upper bodies and legs in profile.[50]

The observations cited above and by other scholars regarding style highlight significant correlations between the bearded heads, the drapery, and the wings of the wind gods and figures from the Pergamon Altar. One only need look at Boreas, Skiron, and Euros to see that they are in the mode of such figures as the snaky-legged giant being attacked by Artemis' dog on the east side and the bull-giant from the south side (Ills. 21a, 21b, 21d, 22, 23).

The disjointed torsion in some of the wind gods, with frontal or nearly frontal upper bodies and legs in profile (see especially Kaikias, Notos, and Zephyros), can be seen much earlier than on the late second-century BC altars on Kos. This stylistic element appears in the Amazonomachy frieze from the Temple of Artemis at Magnesia (Ills. 24, 25),[51] a monument that is dated slightly later than the Pergamon Altar (ca. 150 BC). Certain of the Magnesian figures share other characteristics identified above as existing in the Pergamene and Tower reliefs, such as deeply set eyes, modeled foreheads, classicizing faces, and heavily muscled physiques.[52]

Various styles of boots are the most common type of footwear on the Pergamon Altar[53] and the Magnesian frieze, and boots are the only footwear on the Horologion. Examination of one type of boot, *embades*, on figures from all three monuments provides particularly useful information for narrowing the chronological range of the Tower reliefs.

Early examples of *embades* show them to be a knee-high closed boot with a swollen top that is laced down the front. Flaps folded down and held in place by a garter are the distinguishing feature; whether they are part of the boot or a sock-like inner lining is unclear. *Embades* seem to have been a Thracian design that was intended to shield against the cold, severe weather of the northern climate. They were imported to Athens (along with other forms of Thracian dress) in the mid-sixth century BC,

49. Karanastasi (2014) 194.
50. Lauter (1988) 155–63, esp. 160–62 and n. 46; he suggests the reliefs from the Tower and the Koan altars are products of the same Rhodian workshop.
51. Yaylali (1976) 129.
52. Davesne (1982) figs. 60 and 75.
53. They provide eleven of the nineteen examples of footwear (all worn by the deities) on the Altar; see Morrow (1985) 108.

and a number of examples can be seen on various horsemen in the mid-fifth-century Parthenon frieze.[54]

In the Hellenistic period, *embades* are shorter, reaching only to the lower bulge of the calf muscle. The specific form worn by the wind gods with jagged-edged or (as described by Morrow) pronged-edged socks (*piloi*) are found only on the three monuments under discussion here.[55] Particularly notable is the fact that they are one of two types of footwear, *krepides* and *embades*, worn by males in the Telephos frieze of the Pergamon Altar. These two types, Morrow points out, are signifiers that specify the ethnicities of figures in this relief: Greeks wear *krepides* (a strapped sandal), and males from Asia Minor (Pergamenes/Mysians, i.e., Teuthras and his courtiers and Telephos and his companions) wear *embades*, including one with pronged *piloi* (Ill. 26).[56] Thus, the *embades* functioned to highlight the geographical and genealogical links between the Attalid patrons of the Pergamon Altar and their mythical ancestor, Telephos.[57]

The utilization of *embades* with pronged *piloi* as the only footwear of the wind gods on the Horologion can be seen as having been influenced by the system of ethnic classification employed in the Telephos frieze of the Pergamon Altar as well a as a geographic indicator, for as mentioned previously, the origin of this style of boots is Thrace, the homeland of the winds.[58]

The Amazonomachy frieze from the Temple of Artemis at Magnesia is the third monument on which *embades* with pronged *piloi* can be seen on a variety of figures. They appear there, however, on both Greek warriors and Amazons, with no apparent association to gender or ethnicity (Ills. 24, 25).[59]

The *embades* and *piloi* of the Magnesian figures are smooth and unadorned. The boots of the wind gods are also smooth and unadorned, although the pronged edges of the *piloi* are depicted in the shape of leaves. Many of the boots on the Pergamon Altar, on the other hand, are sculptured with complex designs. Karanastasi focuses on these patterns of adornment, which leads her to find no consistent comparisons between boots on these two monuments. As a result, she rejects the footwear as a means of dating the Tower.[60] Morrow points out, however, that such details as front openings, laces, and decorative patterns were not usually sculptured but were more frequently added in paint.[61] No color has survived on the footwear of either the Octagon or the Temple of

54. Morrow (1985) 65–66, figs. 43–50.
55. Morrow does not include the Horologion in her study. Since she is creating a chronological system based on the structure and temporal changes in the various types of Greek footwear, she relies on information from monuments whose dates are well-defined and generally accepted.
56. Winnefeld (1910) pl. 34.1.
57. Morrow (1985) 136–37.
58. See *Iliad*, Bk. 23.263–264.
59. Davesne (1982) fig. 18 (Block 9, figure 2); figs. 35 and 37 (Block 15, figure 4); figs. 39 and 40 (Block 16, figure 2); figs. 59 and 61(Block 22, figure 4); figs. 71 and 72 (Block 27, figure 2); figs. 103 and 104 (Block #34, figure 1).
60. Karanastasi (2014) 189.
61. Morrow (1985) 65.

Artemis, and it is not possible to know if there were patterned designs on the boots. It should be reiterated that it is not the decorated surface of the boots that is the significant factor here. The pertinent point of comparison is that *embades* with prong-edged *piloi* in the Hellenistic period are found only on the Pergamon Altar, the Magnesian frieze, and the Horologion. This, then, supports a date for the Tower reliefs closer to the middle of the second century BC.

The Construction Date and the Tower's Patron

The Construction Date

Construction of the Tower has been dated variously between the mid-second and late first centuries BC.[62] A convincing argument can be made, however, in support of a date ca. 140 BC, a time of relative peace and prosperity in Athens and a period during which good relations with various Hellenistic monarchs resulted in a number of major donations of prominent monuments to the city. The political and economic environment changed significantly by the early first century BC as a result of chaos caused by the Mithridatic Wars and the assault on Athens by the Roman general Sulla, thus creating an atmosphere that was not conducive to major construction projects.

Analysis of the date is unquestionably inhibited by the dearth of information from ancient sources. The lack of a dedicatory inscription results in a significant gap in our knowledge. One assumes it would have provided the name of the donor, thus possibly leading to the monument's date. The texts of Vitruvius and Varro, while not very comprehensive, do supply evidence regarding the architect. And certain omissions in their commentaries may offer clues as to the condition of the Tower in the first century BC.

Vitruvius's books on architecture were published in the early Augustan period, but he may have seen the Octagon two decades previously on his return journey from Asia Minor to Rome in 47 BC. As Kienast states, Vitruvius's detailed comments on the aspects of the building he discusses are so accurate that it is as though he is standing in front of the Tower.[63] This treatise was preceded by Varro's exposition, *De Re Rustica,*

62. Construction dates (all BC) for the Tower as suggested by various scholars are as follows:

Ca. 165–88:	Smith (1985) [after 166 and before the attack by Sulla]
Ca. 160/150–130/120:	von Freeden (1983) 191; Camp (2001) 178–79; Corso (2009) 318
Probably second century:	Rottländer, et al. (1989) 61–62
Latter half of second century:	Simon, *LIMC* 8.1, 188–89 (*s.v.* "Venti")
Last quarter of second century:	Durm (1910) 506; Lauter (1979) 411; Kienast (2014) 142
End of second/first half of first century:	Hesberg, 1980, 53 [curved consoles in the second interior cornice]
Before 88, possibly second century:	Kienast (1997) 60–61; Ridgway (2002) 52
Mid-first century, (possibly late second):	Stewart (1990), v.1, 231–32
Ca. 100–37:	Robinson (1943) 298–99
Mid- or later first century:	Habicht (1996) 85; Thompson (1987) 6; Robinson (1984), 424.

63. Kienast (2014) 129–30.

written in 37 BC. Book Three, however, which contains references to the Horologion, is a fictional dialogue set in 54 BC, thus giving a *terminus ante quem* in the third quarter of the first century BC. Varro, like Vitruvius, however, also may have seen the building earlier than his written account, perhaps in the years immediately after the Sullan siege on Athens (87/86 BC) when he was studying in the city.[64] This would place the *terminus ante quem* for construction of the Tower early in the first century BC.

In his comprehensive analysis of the architecture of the Horologion, Kienast concludes that it is possible to make only rough arguments in analyzing the construction date because the structural style of the Tower is unique; thus, it is incapable of being assigned a temporal classification. Regarding specific architectural features, he finds no clearly defined chronological categories for any of the Octagon's components. The door frames, lion-head water spouts, and other elements have no close comparisons. Examples he cites suggest a date from the end of the second century to the middle of the first century BC, although he states that the second interior cornice (except for the consoles) follows earlier Pergamene examples.

Consequently, Kienast places most of his focus for determining the date on identifying the *floruit* of the architect, which he bases on the date of a sundial from Tinos, generally accepted to have been made by the Tower's architect.[65] The sundial bears an epigram laudatory in its description of Andronikos' skills, referring to him as a second Eudoxos (founder of the discipline of astronomy) and stating that he calculated the course of the stars. The instrument dates to the last quarter of the second century BC; thus, this is the date Kienast assigns to the Tower. The inscription does not, however, indicate the length of Andronikos' career and so does not preclude the possibility that he may have been near the end of a long and active life when working on Tinos, thereby allowing an earlier date for construction of the Horologion.

The only inscriptions extant from the Tower are the names of the wind gods (*CIG* I, 518). These Kienast describes as carelessly carved, the architectonic marks on the blocks suggesting that they were executed by stonemasons, not a skilled engraver; thus, he believes they cannot be compared with official inscriptions. The differences in the carving quality of the inscriptions cannot be overlooked, but it should be noted that in an earlier article, to which he does not refer in his monograph, Kienast's analysis of the letter forms finds that they differ significantly from well-dated examples from the middle through the late first century BC. He considers them instead to be nearly identical to those in the dedicatory inscription on the architrave of the Stoa of Attalos (*IG* II², 3171), which dates to ca. 140 BC. Von Freeden's evaluation of the inscribed names leads him to support a construction date in the third quarter of the second century BC.[66]

64. Corso (1997) 400; (2009) 314–16.
65. Kienast (2014) 135–38, 140.
66. Von Freeden (1983) 191; Kienast (1997) 61–62, 64 n. 36. Kienast, for example, finds no comparison between letter forms from the Octagon with those in the dedicatory inscription from the Temple of Roma and Augustus on the Acropolis (*IG* II², 3173), which is dated ca. 25 BC.

A date of ca. 140 BC for the Octagon can be supported by an array of evidence. First, in regard to the architecture, the use of mixed orders in the Tower porches and in the interior engaged colonnade is chronologically connotative. This architectural characteristic is common among buildings dating to the middle Hellenistic period, an era that brings back this and other forms found in Archaic architecture (for example, there is a revival of pseudodipteral temples). Among the many examples of structures with mixed orders are the following, which date to the second quarter of the second century BC:

- the stoas in the Sanctuary of Athena at Pergamon with Doric capitals beneath a Doric frieze on the exterior of the lower level, but Ionic columns and capitals beneath a Doric frieze on the upper level;
- the engaged order on the upper walls of the *bouleuterion* at Miletos consisting of column shafts with Ionic fillets and no bases; capitals consisting of a low, square, undecorated abacus; an echinus carved with an egg and dart motif below which was a bead and reel molding; and an entablature consisting of dentils above a triglyph-metope frieze;
- the Milesian storehouse in the south agora, adorned with an engaged colonnade in a mixed order (above a high orthostate course) in which the column shafts and capitals were identical to those on the *bouleuterion;* they supported a friezeless Ionic entablature with two fasciae.[67]

Comparisons between the carving styles and other aspects of the wind gods and figures in the friezes from the Pergamon Altar and the Temple of Artemis at Magnesia as discussed above also support a date closer to the mid-second century BC. The various features evaluated in these images are unruly hair, deep-set eyes, modeled foreheads, classicizing faces, stocky bodies, awkward torsion, style of wing feathers, and footwear.

One can thus conclude from the evidence, that the architect, as unusual as his creation may have been, was influenced in his design by architectural and sculptural tastes exhibited in monuments from the middle of the second century BC. This, then, would allow for a construction date in the third quarter of the second century BC.

The Patron

The unusual shape of the Horologion has inspired debate as to whether the early third-century BC lighthouse at Alexandria, where the second of its three levels was octagonal (Ill. 27), may have influenced the Tower's architect. If so, would this indicate that the Athenian building was paid for by one of the Ptolemies? Several scholars

67. See Knackfuss (1908) figs. 16–22, 30; pls. 8, 9.1, 9.2; Knackfuss (1924) figs. 173, 182–183; pls. 22, 23.189; Schazmann (1923) 40–43, fig. 19; Webb (1996) 57, 102. The Stoa of Attalos in the Greek Agora at Athens also incorporates Doric, Ionic, and palm capitals, but its Ionic capitals are paired with an Ionic frieze.

have suggested that this was the case.[68] Along with the octagonal component in the lighthouse, those who support this hypothesis base it on the following factors: Tritons adorned both buildings; the water-run device inside the Tower was some type of clock, the technology for which likely originated in Alexandria; one of the Ptolemies built a gymnasium in the neighborhood of the Tower in Athens;[69] and there was a well-established relationship between the Ptolemies and the Athenians.

In regard to its design, I think it more likely that the Horologion was not specifically influenced by a single monument. Rather, it is an example of the architectural creativity of the time and was one of the many innovative centralized edifices documented for the early and middle Hellenistic periods. In the mid-fourth century BC, the repertoire of building types expanded beyond temples, altars, treasuries, stoas, and other standard religious and civic buildings (most of which were rectangular) to include monumental tombs, heroa, cult buildings, and commemorative monuments that exhibited a much wider variety in structural composition. Architects working in Asia Minor were particularly important to this process, beginning with those involved in the construction of the Mausoleum at Halicarnassus. This colossal nearly square funerary monument had a high podium (consisting of an estimated three progressively indented levels) crowned by a four-sided colonnade supporting a pyramidal roof. There followed other centralized buildings with engaged or freestanding colonnades on tall lower courses. Examples include the Belevi Mausoleum (a square colonnade on a square podium), the Rotunda of Arsinoe at Samothrace (a tall pseudo two-story tholos with an engaged colonnade on the upper walls), the Heroon of Ptolemy II and Arsinoe II at Limyra (a circular colonnade on a square base), and the Octagon at Ephesus (an octagonal colonnade and high-pitched octagonal roof on a square podium).[70] The Lysicrates Monument in Athens, which has a circular colonnade on a tall square base (Ill. 28) and was built at the eastern foot of the Acropolis in 335/334 BC, is a small choragic dedication that anticipates by half a century the structure of the topmost segment of the Pharos, a circular colonnade on a round base.[71] As for patronage, the Ptolemies certainly were major builders outside their own territory, especially from the late fourth through the third century. Most notable was their largesse to the Sanctuary of the Great Gods at Samothrace in the northern Aegean. In Attica, they fought alongside the Athenians to free the city from Macedonian control, which was accomplished in 229 BC. As a result, several portrait statues of Ptolemies were erected in the Greek Agora, and a statue of Ptolemy III was added to the Monument of the Eponymous Heroes. It may have been at this time that the Macedonian king of Egypt made a gift of a gymnasium to the city.[72]

68. See von Freeden (1983) 66–68, nn. 4–10; 77; Camp (2001) 179.
69. Miller (1995) passim, esp. p. 233, n. 58.
70. Thür (1990) 43–56; Webb (1996) passim, esp. 76–79, 125–26, 147–48, figs. 32, 98, 136, 137.
71. Ridgway (1990) 15–17; La Riche (1996) 82. The Lysicrates Monument is the earliest known structure to place Corinthian columns, which had infrequently adorned the interior of temples, on the exterior of a structure.
72. Camp (2001) 167–68.

Other monarchs made important architectural donations to the city as well, including the Seleucid king Antiochus IV Epiphanes and Ariobarzanes of Cappadocia.[73] Corso, in his analysis of Vitruvius' discussion of Athenian monuments, states that the buildings that most strike him "show the hellenistic taste of Asia Minor at Athens. They are in most cases instances of patronage by Asian kings [such as] the Tower of the Winds."[74]

Since Andronikos was the name that was associated with the building, Kienast suggests it was the architect himself who may have been the donor of the monument. He can offer no specific evidence, however, including how Andronikos might have attained the wealth necessary to fund such a costly venture. Thus, Kienast cautions that his conclusions are theoretical and lead to no confirmed proof.[75] His caution aside, one must reflect on why the Tower was identified with the architect by the three ancient sources instead of with a royal donor. Varro and Vitruvius are not comprehensive in their comments about the building; they are chiefly interested in the fact that eight winds are depicted, which was an unusual number. Varro compares the Tower's frieze to the winds enumerated on his private aviary in Italy, a domed rotunda. Vitruvius lists the winds by name and also mentions the weather vane, but primarily because it functioned in relation to the figured reliefs. Thus, it is not difficult to understand that the creative person who designed the Octagon was of greater importance to these men than the person who financed the project. It is notable as well that in his treatise on architecture, Vitruvius understandably more often lists the names of architects rather than donors.[76]

As stated above, there is no confirmed proof regarding the identity of the donor. There is among the Hellenistic monarchs, however, a king who should be afforded serious consideration—Attalos II. It was the Attalids of Pergamon who were particularly connected to and beneficent toward Athens in the second century BC. Like the Ptolemies, the Attalids under Attalos I were allied with the Athenians in war against the Macedonians. In 200 BC a cult and priesthood were established in his honor, and he was named the eponymous hero of a new tribe (Attalis), honors that were similarly awarded to Ptolemy III. A significant amount of epigraphic evidence attests to the strong and ongoing relationship between Athens and Pergamon throughout the reigns of his successors, Eumenes II and Attalos II.[77]

Athens' urban center was adorned with a number of Attalid buildings and several royal portrait statues (at least some of which may have been gifts of the Athenians).[78]

73. Vitruvius, Bk. 5.9.1, Bk. 7.Introduction.15.
74. Corso (1997) 400. Corso believes that Andronikos was from Kyrrhos in Syria, not Macedonia, thus, he believes that the Octagon was built under the patronage of one of the Seleucid kings.
75. Kienast (2014) 143–45.
76. See, for example, Vitruvius, Bk. 7.Introduction.12–15.
77. Habicht (1990) passim.
78. Vitruvius, Bk. 5.9.1; Pausanias, Bk. 1.25.2; Camp (2001) 171–73; Stewart (2004) passim, esp. 68, 72, 182, 185, 197–200 and nn. 26 and 27, 220, 223, 226, figs. 227 and 228; Camp (2010) 122–23; Kästner (2016) 39; Papini (2016) 41, 43 and nn. 22–25; Karoglou (2016) 63–64.

Along the east flank of the Greek Agora was the elegant Stoa of Attalos II (ca. 140 BC), in front of which was a bronze quadriga on a tall marble pedestal in which stood a portrait statue of the royal donor. Other pillar monuments supporting statues of Pergamene kings stood near the Dipylon Gate and on the west side of the Middle Stoa. On the north side of the passage leading to the Propylaea and at the northeast corner of the Parthenon were bronze chariot groups on tall pedestals, each depicting one of the Attalid monarchs. On the south wall of the Acropolis above the Theater of Dionysus were monumental figures of Eumenes II and Attalos I or II. Also on the south wall was a victory monument, probably dedicated by Attalos I (ca. 200 BC), containing bronze figures in the round that depicted battles against the Giants, the Amazons, the Persians at Marathon, and the Gauls in Mysia. On the south slope of the Acropolis, serving theater patrons, was the great Stoa of Eumenes II (r. 197–159 BC), near which was a portrait of the donor. Because of its strong resemblance to the plan of the library at Pergamon, the Metroön, which was built shortly after the stoa, may also be an Attalid construction.[79]

A suggestion has been put forward that there was a third Attalid stoa that may have stood in the vicinity of the Horologion, most likely on the eastern side of the plaza.[80] If future excavation substantiates its existence, the presence of an edifice built by Attalos II in the neighborhood of the Octagon would lend support to the proposal that the Pergamene king was the patron of the Tower. This hypothesis is based on numerous extant remains of Doric elements (columns, epistyle blocks, triglyphs, and cornice blocks) and Ionic elements (cornices, column drums, and column bases) that may have originally been components of Hellenistic stoas damaged during the siege of Athens by the Herulians. The Doric components were found on the Acropolis, where they had been reused in the cella of the Parthenon when the great temple was repaired after having suffered a fire in the third or fourth century AD.[81] The Ionic components, apparently not having been reused, were found in the entrance to the Library of Hadrian and in the area of the Roman Agora. Dinsmoor was the first to classify the Doric columns as second-century BC Pergamene in style. Travlos, in agreement with him, reconstructed them as a large two-story stoa (ca. 170–180 meters long) with semi-fluted Doric columns on the lower level and double Ionic columns on the upper level, deeming the entirety of the building to be in the same style as the Stoa of Eumenes and the Stoa of Attalos. Korres has challenged Travlos' claim that the Doric and Ionic elements come from a single monument. He suggests there were at least two other stoas somewhere in Athens similar to those of Eumenes and Attalos II, and perhaps a third in the form of a single-storey Doric stoa in the area east of the Roman Agora.

79. Habicht (1990) 574 and n. 74.

80. Dinsmoor (1934) 102; Travlos (1971) 281, 444; Travlos (1973) 218–36; Korres (1996) 143–44, nn. 36 and 37, figs. 5 and 7; Kienast (2014) 24–25 and nn. 118–120; Greco (2014) 762–65, fig. 427.

81. Travlos (1971) 444–45.

The deep bond between the Attalid royal family and Athens began in the early decades of the Pergamene dynasty. During the reigns of Eumenes I (r. 263–241 BC) and Attalos I (r. 241–197 BC), large sums of money were given to Lycon, the head of the Peripatetic School in Athens. Pergamon's connection with the Academy, where Attalos I financed the planting of its garden, was even stronger.[82] Between the last quarter of the third century through the first quarter of the second century, three heads of the school were from Pergamon, philosophers who had been students there themselves. In the first quarter of the second century, Eumenes II and his three brothers traveled several times to Athens to participate in the Panathenaic Games, where they triumphed in the chariot races; the horses of Attalos II ran to victory more than once in the festival.[83]

Attalos II (r. 159–138 BC) made a number of visits to Athens over the decades, the first in 192 BC, and lived in the city when he was a student at the Academy. It is he whom I consider most plausible as the patron of the Tower. One may ask why the Horologion, so different from other Pergamene benefactions, may have attracted the sponsorship of this monarch. The answer may lie in the fact that the Attalid kings were great patrons of the arts and sciences. Their support for education is reflected in the gymnasium complex at Pergamon, the largest known from antiquity, and in large donations to other cities—along with Athens—for gymnasia, teachers, and resident scholars. Their court was a dynamic center for academics from a wide field of intellectual pursuits, among which were sculpture, architecture, astronomy, mathematics, and engineering.[84] The most important resident scholar during the reigns of Eumenes II and Attalos II was Krates, head of the renowned library at Pergamon. Krates' belief that Earth was a sphere led him to fashion the first globe, which was said to have been ten feet in diameter.[85] His view of the gods was that they were allegorical forces of nature. One can see how such a scholar may have influenced Attalos' decision to sponsor the Horologion.

With no dedicatory inscription extant, it is not possible to know for certain whether construction of the Tower was funded by the Athenians themselves or by a foreign donor. If the building was a gift from a Hellenistic king, however, several factors speak in favor of Attalos II as the Tower's most likely patron. These include epigraphic evidence attesting to the history of Attalid support for the city, primarily in the second century BC; the great respect that various members of the royal family had for the culture and educational institutions of Athens; the numerous monuments in second-century BC Athens depicting or donated by Attalos II and other Pergamene kings; similarities between the dedicatory inscription on the Stoa of Attalos and the names of the wind gods on the Octagon; parallels in stylistic and other details between figured

82. Diogenes Laertius 5.67.

83. Their participation occurred in 186, 182, or 178 BC. See Hansen (1971) 105 and n. 113, 395–97; Habicht (1990) 568–69, 573.

84. Hansen (1971) 390, 395, 397–433.

85. Strabo Bk. 2.5.10 (C 116).

reliefs from Pergamon and the Tower; and the fact that this was a city of particular import to Attalos II, in which he had lived and where he had been educated.

The Water-Run Mechanism

The existence of carved hour lines for sundials[86] on the exterior of the monument and information from Vitruvius regarding a Triton weather vane on the roof clearly define certain functions of the Hellenistic building as those of an horologion and weather station. The interior presents no such clarity regarding use. Holes in the floors of both chambers that connect to an underground channel, the groove for a water pipe in the south wall of the annex, and the shelf in the annex provide evidence for some type of mechanism driven by the controlled flow of water under pressure from a holding tank. Two proposals have been offered for what the device may have been: (a) a water clock and (b) a celestial globe (orrery).

In their 1762 publication on the Tower of the Winds, Stuart and Revett propose that the it housed the components of a mechanized water clock, although they did not attempt to reconstruct the instrument.[87] Theirs is a reasonable suggestion, for the collection of reliable information about time and weather in order to facilitate commercial trade, various civic affairs, and religious festivals was important to the daily life of Athenians.

The technology for chronometry had been greatly enhanced by the early third century BC, when mechanisms to automate water clocks were first designed. Previously, time was measured by a simpler form of nonmechanized water clock, the clepsydra. This device consisted of two containers, one standing at a higher level than the other. Water flowed at a controlled rate through a hole in the upper vessel into the vessel below. The lower container had marks along its side indicating the hours at the various water levels. A large public clepsydra, which had a square stone tank approximately two meters deep, had been constructed in the Greek Agora abutting the northwest wall of the Aiakeion in the second half of the fourth century BC. It was demolished when land was cleared for the erection of the Middle Stoa ca. 140 BC. As a result, Athenians would no longer have had access to a monumental water clock in the city center, something on which they no doubt had depended for two centuries.[88] Thus, there would have been a need for a public timekeeping device.

86. For discussion of the forms and functions of the various types of sundials and gnomons, see Evans (1999) 243–51, 270–72. For detailed analysis of the sundials on the Tower of the Winds, see Schaldach (2014) 197–226.

87. Stuart and Revett (1762), ch. 3, 13–25, esp. 15–16; Stuart and Revett (1825) 41.

88. Thompson (1954) 37–38; Thompson and Wycherley (1972) 65, 202; Armstrong and Camp (1977) 147–61; Camp (2010) 170–73, figs. 127, 130 (this 1969 illustration designates the Aiakeion as the "law court"). Von Freeden (1983) 192–94, suggests that even with the construction of the Middle Stoa accommodations could have been made allowing the clepsydra to continue in place.

Noble and Price expand on the hypothesis of the Dilettanti and present a detailed reconstruction of a clock regulated by water piped to it from two tanks (one on the floor and the other on the shelf) located in the annex of the Tower (Ill. 29b). Taking into account the types of mechanisms extant in the Hellenistic period, they suggest the most likely would be the anaphoric clock described by Vitruvius, the technology for which may have been devised by the astronomer Hipparchos in the mid-second century BC.[89] The major component of an anaphoric clock was a large bronze disk engraved with a map of the stars and constellations (between the North Pole and the Tropic of Capricorn). Noble and Price believe that the device may have been similar to one dating to the first or second century AD whose remains were found in Roman ruins near Salzburg, Austria.[90] That instrument is reconstructed with a disk approximately 1.25 meters in diameter weighing approximately ninety pounds.

Noble and Price suggest that in the Horologion the disk would have been attached to an axle with a counterweight that was supported by the central column in the main chamber. The axle would have been turned by a bronze chain wrapped around it whose movement was controlled by a float in the lower tank in the annex. As the water level in the lower tank rose, supplied by the tank on the shelf, the float would rise and the counterweight would descend, thus turning the axle at one rotation per day. A network of bronze wires, suspended from the two flanking columns and hanging in front of the rotating disk, would have displayed the hours. Noble and Price suggest that statues may have stood atop the columns, perhaps Poseidon in the center with Heracles and Atlas at either side holding the wire grid in front of the rotating bronze disk (Ill. 29a). When the disk turned on its axle at a controlled rate, its position behind the network of reference wires indicated the time.

As described by Noble and Price, the functions of the Octagon's mechanism were astronomical and astrological as well as chronometric. "The anaphoric disc is therefore very similar in character to the well-known astrolabe. . . . [T]he anaphoric clock, in addition to telling the time, gave a quite theatrical simulation of the known universe." This idea was supported by Travlos, who referred to the building as "possibly even a planetarium." Price broadens the meaning of such complex devices by stating that "It would be a mistake to suppose that water-clocks, or the sundials to which they are closely related, had the primary utilitarian purpose of telling the time. Doubtless they were on occasion made to serve this practical end, but on the whole their design and intention seems to have been the aesthetic or religious satisfaction derived from making a device to simulate the heavens."[91]

89. Vitruvius Bk. 9.8.8–15. Noble and Price (1968) 351–53,pl. 118.

90. Evans (1999) 251–56 and n. 27, figs. 12a, 12b, 13; Eibner (2013) 177–83. See also Vitruvius, Book 9, where he discusses the zodiac, planets, phases of the moon, the course of the sun through the twelve signs, and constellations. The Greeks' system for timekeeping divided the day into two periods (sunlight and darkness) with the period of sunlight divided into twelve equal segments or hours. This resulted in longer hours during summer and shorter hours during winter.

91. Price (1964) 13; Noble and Price (1968) 352; Travlos (1971) 281.

Kienast rejects the reconstruction of the mechanism as any type of clock for several reasons: the amount of water supplied by the system would have been far greater than necessary for a clock; the water pressure that is indicated by the height of the tank on the shelf and the sizes of the pipes is too great; the water tank for a clock would properly have been at ground level or below ground level; and the system of three freestanding columns supporting an axle, a large bronze disk, and a network of wires would not have offered enough physical stability. He also notes that ancient water clocks stood either in the open or under a roofed structure so as to be easily seen by passersby. In order to view a clock in the Tower, a visitor would have had to enter a windowless room lit only indirectly through its two entrance doors.[92]

Kienast finds no unambiguous solution to the problem of defining the type of instrument that was on display in the octagonal chamber. He notes that the holes and grooves in the floors and walls provide insufficient evidence on which to base an accurate reconstruction, and without additional evidence, any answers remain in the realm of the hypothetical. Consequently, he omits a water-run device from his primary illustration of the reconstructed monument.[93] He does, however, propose a different mechanism from that presented by Noble and Price.

Kienast takes into consideration that water was collected in a tank raised approximately two meters above floor level on the elevated platform in the annex; consequently, the water pressure was relatively high. According to his analysis of the piping system, the continuous flow of water emerged from the central aperture in the main chamber where the pipe then trifurcated, sending water spouting straight up and to the two lateral columns. Such high water pressure indicates that it must have operated a complex mechanism capable of performing intricate tasks. That the device was valued and well cared for is demonstrated by the Octagon's lockable doors, which were necessary to keep the mechanism safe and to protect it from inclement weather.

In speculating on the type of device within the building, Kienast suggests that Andronikos viewed the entire Tower as a symbol of cosmic order. Citing the transition from octagonal chamber to hemispherical ceiling with its depiction of the heavens, the architectonic framework thus would have supported an apparatus that had a relationship to the cosmos. Consequently, he expands on the suggestion by Noble and Price that an astronomical function was a feature of the mechanism and proposes that the chamber housed not a water clock but an orrery, a celestial globe.[94] Thus, the Horologion, as was suggested previously by Travlos, would have served as a planetarium. This hypothesis would be in keeping with the description of the interior of the Tower by the Turkish traveler Evliya Çelebi, who describes astrological and astronomical images representing the zodiac and various celestial bodies arrayed across twelve compartments on the domed ceiling.[95]

92. Kienast (2014) 121–23.
93. Kienast (2014) 128, pl. 40.
94. Kienast (1993) 271–75; Kienast (2014) 121–28; fig. 164.
95. Mackay (1969) 468; Dankoff & Kim (2010) 289.

Literary evidence mentioning celestial globes dates at least as early as and perhaps earlier than the fourth century BC. The earliest extant detailed description of such a device is provided by the third-century BC poem *Phaenomena* by Aratus, who lived in Soli in southern Anatolia. In his verses, Aratus supplies the principal elements portrayed on such a sphere: (a) circles depicting the zodiac, the equator, and the tropics; and (b) the names of the constellations, on which circle they lie, and their relationship to one another.

The oldest extant tangible celestial sphere is part of a sculpture called the Farnese Atlas in the Museo Nazionale in Naples in which it is held by a figure of the sky-supporting Titan of Greek myth (Ill. 30). This is not a functioning scientific device; it is a marble representation of a celestial globe dating to the first or second century AD and is generally considered to be a Roman copy of an original Hellenistic work. Its importance lies in the fact that it displays features described by Aratus.[96] Three circles surround the upper half of the globe, the central ring depicting the yearlong path of the sun. Constellations represented on the sphere include Taurus, Gemini, Cancer, Leo, Canis Major, Argo, Hydra, and Orion, among others. Also delineated are the celestial equator, the Tropic of Capricorn, and the Tropic of Cancer. A description of a scientific celestial globe provided by the early second-century AD Alexandrian astronomer and mathematician Ptolemy includes the fact that the sphere should be dark in color to represent the night sky and that most stars should be yellow except for those few that appear to be red.[97]

Kienast suggests that the Tower mechanism may have consisted of a globe of the heavens in the form of an armillary sphere supported by a large bronze cylindrical stand.[98] The armillary sphere, unlike the celestial globe, is not solid; it is composed of bronze rings welded together at diverse angles that depict the principal circles, including the path of the sun, the equator, the Tropic of Cancer, and the Tropic of Capricorn. Like the celestial globe, the armillary sphere dates as early as the fourth century BC, for a description can be found in Plato's *Timaios* (36B–D). While no ancient armillary spheres are extant, a wall painting at Stabiae includes a depiction of the device.[99]

As for how a scientific celestial sphere may have been displayed in the Horologion, Kienast suggests the mechanism was similar to the orrery that was devised by Archimedes and described by Cicero:

> Gaius Sulpicius Gallus happened to be at the house of Marcus Marcellus. . . . [H]e ordered the celestial globe to be brought out which the grandfather of Marcellus had carried off from Syracuse, when that very rich and beautiful city was taken, though he

96. Schaefer (2005) believes the constellations on the Farnese Atlas are derived from Hipparchus' lost star catalog created ca. 129 BC.

97. Evans (1999) 239–41 and nn. 8–10, fig. 2.

98. Kienast (2014) 127–28, fig. 165.

99. Evans (1999) 241–43, 277–79 and n.14, figs. 3, 28; (an illustration of a mosaic from Casa di Leda at Soluntum in which is depicted an armillary with a Wind god displayed in each of the four corners); Kienast (2014) 127, fig. 164.

> took home with him nothing else out of the great store of booty captured. Though I had heard this globe mentioned quite frequently on account of the fame of Archimedes, when I actually saw it I did not particularly admire it; for that other celestial globe, also constructed by Archimedes, which the same Marcellus placed in the temple of Virtue, is more beautiful as well as more widely known among the people. But when Gallus began to give a very learned explanation of the device, I concluded that the famous Sicilian had been endowed with greater genius than one would imagine it possible for a human being to possess. For Gallus told us that the other kind of celestial globe, which was solid and contained no hollow space, was a very early invention, the first one of that kind having been constructed by Thales of Miletus, and later marked by Eudoxus of Cnidus (a disciple of Plato, it was claimed) with the constellations and stars which are fixed in the sky. He also said that many years later Aratus, borrowing this whole arrangement and plan from Eudoxus, had described it in verse, without any knowledge of astronomy, but with considerable poetic talent. But this newer kind of globe, he said, on which were delineated the motions of the sun and moon and of those five stars which are called wanderers, or, as we might say, rovers, contained more than could be shown on the solid globe, and the invention of Archimedes deserved special admiration because he had thought out a way to represent accurately by a single device for turning the globe those various and divergent movements with their different rates of speed. And when Gallus moved the globe, it was actually true that the moon was always as many revolutions behind the sun on the bronze contrivance as would agree with the number of days it was behind it in the sky. Thus the same eclipse of the sun happened on the globe as would actually happen, and the moon came to the point where the shadow of the earth was at the very time when the sun . . . [was] out of the region (trans. Keyes).[100]

Regarding how the mechanism may have functioned in the Tower, Kienast states that it is not possible to specify the details of how water emerged from the central aperture to supply power to move the components of the instrument. One can presume that the water traveled through a system of gears, although how many or what the gears looked like Kienast does not venture to guess. In the center of the framework of rings would have been Earth turning on its axis. He thinks the mechanism would have filled much of the space within the area circumscribed by the balustrade ("auf den Ring der Balustrade abgestimmt gewesen sein")[101]—that is, approximately three meters in diameter—and would have reached to between the first and second cornices. He refrains from speculating how water was drained away, whether in a visible or closed system; he does, however, note the significant erosion of the marble floor slabs.

Kienast ponders the relationship between certain features of the building and the possible design of the apparatus: the height of the chamber, the elaborate cornice above the second zone, the octagonal shape of the room, the domed ceiling, the management of light in the chamber, and the painted motifs on the ceiling. He analyzes the ground plan of the structure, which he demonstrates was created by squares drawn inside one

100. Cicero, *De Republica* 1.21–22 (trans. Keyes, 1928).
101. Kienast (2014) 127.

another.[102] The resulting construction lines lead to the twelve astrologic houses and indicate from that the twelve constellations—a connection that surely is not due to chance. Most important was the transition from octagonal to round forms, which was very expensive to execute and was attained only through extremely complicated construction methods. The number eight is displayed throughout the entire building and can be explained mostly on the basis of the major celestial bodies known at that time—Mercury, Mars, Venus, Jupiter, Saturn, the sun, the moon, and the fixed star.

Kienast expands his argument significantly beyond the hypothetical reconstruction of the water-run device when he concludes that if the transformation from octagonal building to round dome was carried out to symbolize the heavens, then the Octagon as an entity has meaning and is of fundamental significance. It cannot be doubted that Andronikos wanted the Tower to be understood as a symbol of the cosmic order. This view supports earlier observations by Price, who also considers the Tower to be an architectural representation of "an interlocking set of theories covering virtually all creation"[103]

Kienast also reflects on the importance of the wind gods and how they fit into the cosmic theme. There is no need for ornate figured reliefs on this building. The sculptured frieze could just as easily have been a simple motif, such as a garland. This means that the wind gods are not only decorative but also determine the form of the Tower and give it additional meaning. These large and carefully made figures are the most elaborate wind cycle from antiquity. Kienast considers their possible connection to Aristotle's theory of elements and antimonies. The four elements would be Earth/Kaikias, air/Euros, water/Lips, and fire/Skiron, and the four antinomies would be hot/Zephyros, cold/Boreas, humid/Notos, and dry/Apeliotes. Thus, they too are to be viewed as an important aspect of world order, an allegory for the cosmos.

The Horologion as a Cultic and Commemorative Monument

The Cult of the Wind Gods and the Importance of Boreas to the Athenians

The Tower of the Winds has not previously been viewed as having a religious function. The above discussion, however, lays the groundwork for proposing here that the Hellenistic structure was more than a weather station (wind vane), chronometer (sundials), and repository for a water-run mechanism. A case will be made that it served at the time of its construction as a cult site for Boreas (and to a lesser extent his brothers) and commemorated his role in the Athenian defeat of the Persian Navy in 480 BC.[104]

102. Kienast (2014) 107–19, 124–25, figs. 147–161, 163.
103. Price (1976) 78–80.
104. In this way, the Horologion echoes Greek theaters, which were both civic structures and sanctuaries for the god Dionysus, thus fitting the pattern of divine sanction sought for civic function. One might also think of the Bouleuterion in the Greek Agora, which housed altars to Zeus Boulaios and Athena Boulaia; see Hansen (1999) 252 and nn. 79 and 80.

Neither Vitruvius nor Varro characterizes the Horologion as a cult site, and neither describes the interior mechanism, which one imagines must have been the central feature of the building in the second century BC. Their comments, in fact, are decidedly not comprehensive descriptions of the unusual edifice but are concentrated instead on the unusual number of winds. In assessing their limited focus, it is important to remember that if they saw the Tower in person it would have been during the period after the attack on the city by Sulla when, on the basis of the Augustan decree, the building seems to have fallen into private hands and must have performed a different function.

The question as to whether Andronikos created an artistic program that unified the Tower's embellishments—sculpture, painting, engaged colonnade, illumination of the ceiling, hydraulic display—is an important consideration. The blue paint and indentations from applied figures on the domed ceiling, along with Evliya's description, make it clear that the representation of the heavens reflected a cosmic motif. While one should not overlook the fact that an octagon supplied multiple surface areas for the creation of vertical sundials, which would have been of special interest to Andronikos, the fact remains that designing an edifice on which eight deities were to be displayed in a prominent frieze on the exterior of the monument attests to the gods' significance. Not only was the depiction of eight winds exceptional, but as discussed previously, the gods as an allegory for world order are an important part of the building's thematic scheme.

The personification of Boreas, the king of the winds, is in the most conspicuous position—the center of the north side of the building. The two flanking pedimented porches on the northeast and northwest walls would have further accentuated his location. Such emphasis is not surprising, for the north wind held great significance for Athenians. According to local legend, as recounted by Herodotus (Bk.7.189), Boreas kidnapped and married Erechtheus' daughter, Oreithyia, whom he saw dancing on the banks of the Ilissus River. In consequence of his marriage to the daughter of the ancient king, the Athenians referred to the wind god as their "son-in-law".[105] Boreas' most important role in Athenian history took place in 480 BC, when prayers and sacrifices were made to the deity asking for his help in defeating Xerxes' navy during the Greco-Persian Wars. After aiding in the destruction of the Persian fleet and delivering a great victory to the Athenians, the cult of the north wind was rewarded with an altar placed near the Ilissus.[106] The Delphians, also alarmed at the prospect of the Greeks confronting the powerful Persian Navy, beseeched Apollo for advice. They were told to pray to all the wind gods for help. As a consequence, they built an altar dedicated to Boreas and his brothers in the shrine of the nymph Thyia at Delphi, and there they made prayers and sacrifices. After the war, many of the floating remains of the Persian warships were blown by the west wind (Zephyros) to the shores of Cape Colias, southeast of Athens. The first fruits of this booty were sent as a thank offering to Delphi.

105. Pindar, *Pythian* 4.182; Robertson (1996) 58–59.

106. Herodotos Bk. 7.189; Plato, *Phaedrus,* 229; Pausanias Bk. 1.19.6. A likely place for the altar of Boreas in Athens is south of the east end of the Temple of Olympian Zeus, at the source of the Callirrhoe spring; see Wycherley (1978) 171.

From these was made a statue twelve cubits tall, which held in its hand the curved stern (*aphlaston*) of a ship.[107]

The wind cult is much older than the late Archaic period, however, as it is attested in prehistoric Greece. Through the centuries, the beneficence of the wind gods was considered to be important not just in war but also for many aspects of daily life, including agriculture, commercial shipping (estimating the arrival date of a ship at sea), and religion (to carry off the smoke of sacrifices to the gods).[108]

Numerous literary and historical references to the wind gods assist in illuminating the nature of their powers. The earliest appear in the poems of Homer. For example, Boreas breathes life into the body of the slain Sarpedon (*Iliad,* Bk. 5.692–698). And at the funeral of Patroclus when the pyre will not burn, Achilles beseeches Boreas and Zephyros to come to his aid. Iris wings her way to their home in Thrace and pleads his case. The two wind gods fly to Troy, and as they feed the fire by blowing through the night, Achilles soaks the ground with libations of wine poured from a golden goblet and a golden bowl (*Iliad* Bk. 23.223–266).[109]

Hesiod divides the winds into two groups based on whom he names as their parents. Boreas, Zephyros, and Notos, as the children of the deities Astraeus and Eos, he defines as salutary winds. The other winds, as the children of the monster Typhon, are described as fierce and deadly.[110]

The winds are frequently presented as chthonic deities. For example, Boreas was depicted as snake-footed on the Chest of Cypselus at Olympia. Aeschylus refers to Zephyros as being born of the earth. In a later source, the winds are described in their homeland, Thrace, as roaring out of a *bothros.* Hampe notes that the winds were viewed as being both Earth-bound and possessing a heavenly nature. As a result, they were honored with sacrifices made at altars and by libations poured into *bothroi,* in a manner similar to the worship of heroes.[111]

Among several brief references to wind cults, Pausanias merely lists the Altar of Zephyros by the Cephissus River near the Sanctuary of Demeter at Eleusis (Bk. 1.37.1) and the Altar to the Winds in Coroneia (Bk. 9.34.2). For the cult at Titane in the Corinthia (Bk. 2.12.1), however, he provides an overview of the rituals performed: the priest sacrificed at the altar once a year, at night; he sang incantations in which he invoked the name of Medea; and he carried out a secret rite designed to appease the wind gods, which involved libations at four *bothroi.* Whether this description of

107. Herodotus Bk. 7.178; Bk. 8.96, 121.

108. Hampe (1967) 7–14; Coppola (2010) passim. In the *Anabasis* (Bk. 4.5.4) Xenophon states that when the ten thousand soldiers were crossing the Armenian highlands and were caught in a storm, they were advised by a seer to sacrifice to the wind gods. In Aristophanes' *The Frogs* (847–848), a black ewe is sacrificed to the winds in order to stave off a typhoon.

109. The wind gods also appear in the *Odyssey;* for example they are important players in the story of Aeolus (Bk. 10.19–94).

110. Hesiod, *Theogony,* 379–380, 869–870.

111. Pausanias Bk. 5.19.1, 9.34.2. Aeschylus, *Agamemnon,* 691. Dionysophanes in Schol. Apoll. Rhod. I 826. Hampe, 9–11 and nn. 9 and 14.

a ritual that took place in the second century AD reflects practices carried out in the Hellenistic period is not known. These elements of wind worship, however—magical hymns, an altar, and *bothroi*—are similar to those found in mystery cults and hero cults.

A case can be made that the water that facilitated the function of the mechanism in the Horologion was itself sacred. Because it flowed into the annex on the south side of the Tower, the likely source was the Clepsydra, the sacred spring on the north slope of the Acropolis. The importance of the Clepsydra to the mythic history of Athens is highlighted by Pausanias (Bk. 1.28.4): "If you go down not into the city but below the formal entrance [Propylaea], you come to a water-spring near a cave sanctuary of Apollo. This is where they believe Apollo mated with Erechtheus' daughter, Kreousa." The spring is mentioned in a number of literary accounts that clearly consider the water to be hallowed. In *Lysistrata,* Aristophanes writes: "How shall I make myself pure to ascend the mount? Very easily, surely, bathe in the Clepsydra."[112] In his biography of Mark Antony, Plutarch states that as the Roman general prepared to set out for war, he took a garland from the sacred olive tree and, in obedience to a certain oracle, filled a vessel with water from the Clepsydra to carry with him.[113]

For the Athenians, the Clepsydra functioned as both a sacred and secular water source. An interesting and unambiguous example of such a custom, albeit from Late Antiquity, is attested at Philippi in the complex that housed the conjoined Hellenistic heroon (whose cult was still active) and the Basilica of St. Paul. There water flowed first through the city's public baths and then into the church baptistery, at which point it was considered to have changed from profane to holy.[114]

The Architectural Structure of Cultic and Commemorative Monuments

The question now to be broached is whether the Tower, whose architectural form has frequently been described as unique, can be classified architecturally as a Hellenistic cult building.

When considering Greek religious architecture one thinks primarily of temples, which are constructed in a somewhat limited variety of forms. Most commonly they are single-storey, rectangular, pedimented structures, often with a pronaos, cella, and opisthodomos enclosed within a peristyle. There are variants, however. Some have columns only across the front and rear. Smaller edifices may omit the rear chamber or the rear chamber and the lateral colonnades. A few temples are round. Almost all face east, although the Temple of Apollo at Bassae lies on a north-south axis, and the temples of his sister Artemis commonly face west. Even with such variations, however, it is generally possible to identify Greek structures as temples by taking note of their form and their orientation.

112. Pausanias Bk. 1.28.4. Aristophanes, *Lysistrata,* 909–911. See also, Aristophanes, *The Wasps,* 857; *The Birds,* 1694.

113. Plutarch, *Life of Antony,* 34.1.

114. See Appendix 3; also Koukouli-Chrysanthaki and Bakirtzis (1995) 49, 56–57; Verhoef (2008) 704,707.

Hellenistic architecture incorporates a separate category of religious buildings—cultic and commemorative monuments—in which many of the edifices so classified are not only structurally different from most other Greek buildings but share among themselves certain specific characteristics. In summary, they are often:

centralized structures—round, square, nearly square, or a combination (e.g., a circular colonnade on a square podium);
tall buildings that are, or appear to be, composed of two (or more) storeys;
adorned with a colonnade on the upper level and either consist of more than one storey, with a freestanding or engaged colonnade on the upper level, or are tall single-storey structures with a freestanding or engaged colonnade (on the exterior and/or interior) along the upper walls, which gives the appearance of upper and lower levels;[115]
laid out on or near a north-south axis, as the topography allows.

Among such cultic and commemorative monuments are the Lion Tomb at Cnidus, the Belevi Mausoleum, the Octagon at Ephesus, and, in the Sanctuary of the Great Gods on Samothrace, the Rotunda of Arsinoe and the Doric Rotunda.

The Horologion is a tall north-facing centralized structure whose walls are demarcated into horizontal sectors, the upper interior of which is adorned with an engaged colonnade. Thus, while the Tower is unique in many respects, it shares these structural features with a number of monuments from the fourth century BC through the Hellenistic period that are classified as cultic or commemorative, and it can be placed alongside the buildings in this category. Kienast, who believes that the Tower performs no religious function, does make note of similarities between the Octagon and other buildings in this group. He acknowledges that the Tower's centralized form is comparable only to heroa and monumental tombs such as the Lion Tomb at Cnidus and the Mausoleum at Halicarnassus. Kienast thinks that the Tower's inner room is clearly patterned after these building types, recalling a Macedonian tomb chamber as well as the dome in a Mycenaean tholos tomb. He also notes that the interior columns, while performing no structural function, are the distinguishing feature not only of Zone 4 but also of the entire inner chamber. He resolutely concludes, however, that the Tower is not a temple, heroon, or tomb.[116]

A third cult building from the sanctuary at Samothrace, the Hieron, although not a centralized edifice, provides an interesting comparison to the Tower in regard to its wall structure and interior colonnade. The Hieron, which is believed to have accommodated certain of the initiation rites into the mysteries of the Great Gods, was a

115. Certain *bouleuteria,* such as in Miletus and Priene, are tall single-storey buildings with some form of colonnade along the upper walls. The architectural form of these civic structures, however, is determined by their functional requirements as assembly halls, which include windows on the upper walls above the highest tiers of seats and, for those that are built into a hillside, access through doors on the upper level.

116. Kienast (2014) 50, 54, 138 and n. 480, 143–44.

north-facing, prostyle, rectangular building that externally resembled a temple.[117] The exterior walls were constructed in a manner similar to those of the Horologion, with four horizontal sections consisting of high ashlar courses divided by narrow headers. These architectural divisions were reflected in the stuccoed interior walls, which were articulated further by different-colored paints: the lowest section was black, the second section was red, and the third section was white. Especially notable was the use at the fourth level of an engaged miniature Doric colonnade, similar to the one found in the Tower of the Winds.[118]

The reasons why many cultic and commemorative monuments were designed with walls comprising distinct superimposed zones and why they were situated with a general or specific north-south orientation are not readily apparent. Considering their functions, however, I think the horizontal wall divisions may have been intended to create an architectural environment that indicated the physical separation between the world of living mortals and the world of deities and the heroic dead. Included in this meaning would be the suggestion of the possibility for a human being to move from one realm to the other—a visual representation of the concept of Ἄγοδος. Thus, the divisions may symbolize different "geographic" spheres; that is, the lowest level denote the earthly province, while the uppermost level ornamented with a colonnade denotes the realm of gods, demigods, and heroes. The placement of the wind gods at the same level as the colonnade on the Tower can be viewed as supporting this idea.[119]

Understanding the significance of these buildings' orientation also presents a challenge. One possibility I offer tentatively for why most face in a northerly direction may be an allusion to the myth of the Hyperboreans, who lived in a blessed place of eternal sun located somewhere far beyond the home of the north wind. Pliny the Elder provides the following description: "Behind these [Ripaean] mountains and beyond the north wind there dwells (if we can believe it) a happy race of people called the Hyperboreans, who live to extreme old age and are famous for legendary marvels. Here are believed to be the hinges on which the firmament turns and the extreme limits of the revolutions of the stars. . . . It is a genial region, with a delightful climate and exempt from every harmful blast. . . . All discord and all sorrow is unknown."[120]

The myth of the Hyperboreans and Pliny's portrayal of their land could be seen to

117. The interior was organized quite differently from the standard Greek temple. It had low two-tiered platforms for benches on the long walls, a *bothros* near the entrance, and a hearth (*eschara*) in the center of the floor.

118. Lehmann (1969) passim, esp. 126–28, 140, pl. 105; McCredie (1992) passim, esp. 239–41, fig. 147; Webb (1996) 76, 121, 144, 147–48, figs. 32, 94, 132, 136, 137; Lehmann (1998) 62–70, 79–86; Ridgway (2002) 20, 22, Ill. 2.

119. Even though Kienast sees no religious function for the Horologion, he does reflect on the purpose of the interior wall divisions, wondering whether the lowest zone might have been considered the region of the visitor, the second zone provided a framework for the mechanism, and the third zone emphasized the height of the chamber leading up to the circular region with miniature columns and the painted domed ceiling; see Kienast (2014) 105.

120. Pliny, *NH* Bk. 4.12.88–89 (trans. H. Rackham).

be reflected in this particular monument for the following reasons. Boreas, the deified personification of the north wind, is in the most prominent position on the Horologion, and the phrase "the hinges on which the firmament turns and the extreme limits of the revolutions of the stars" calls to mind the interior of the Tower, where images of the zodiac and celestial bodies were arrayed across the domed ceiling.

One final architectural feature merits examination in light of the previous discussion. The floor block at the center of the octagonal chamber, which contains the large aperture, is an anomaly. It is eight-sided but is not a regular octagon in that the sides and angles are not equal. This elongated irregular polygon is approximately 2 meters in length, 0.75 meters wide on the ends, and 1.50 meters wide at its midsection. The unavoidable question is therefore: Since this centralized octagonal building is so consistent in its other geometric forms, why is the central floor block elongated and irregular? There is no obvious answer.

The effect produced by this lengthened slab on a viewer is that it transfers emphasis from the centralized aspects of the architectural plan to the north-south axis. This would have been accentuated further by the three columns standing on the south side. Considering the precision and sophistication of the building's design, one can only assume that the shape of the central floor block performed a specific function. Is it possible that it reflects the contour of an object that stood on it or above it? If it does, what would have had a similar shape? The only object that comes to mind is a boat.

The following discussion is intended to supply a hypothetical assessment of the Tower's thematic program, which may have included a depiction of a boat. While the evidence is insufficient to result in a clear resolution of the problem, there are questions that need to be acknowledged even if they cannot be answered with certainty.

Public display of ships in a variety of forms was common in the Hellenistic period. Some were actual warships offered as votives in sanctuaries, such as those in the Neorion at Samothrace and the Hall of the Bulls at Delos.[121] This was a practice that goes back to an earlier time, however. Herodotus (8.121.1) relates that three Phoenician warships from the Battle of Salamis were dedicated in sanctuaries at Isthmia, Sounion, and Salamis. Other displays included ships that were part of a sculptured work of art, such as the Naval Monument at Cyrene and the Nike of Samothrace (Ill. 31).[122] The reason for including a ship in such dedications is usually self-evident even if specific details are not always known. They are associated with victory in battle, safety at sea, and other maritime-related themes. If a ship was part of the display inside the Tower, one should look for a similar motivation.

121. Neorion: Lehmann (1998) 109–111, figs. 49–52; Wescoat (2005) 153–172. Hall of the Bulls: Webb (1996) 134–36, figs. 110–115; Vlachou (2010) 71–80.

122. Cyrene: Ridgway (1990) 215–16, pl. 99. Nike of Samothrace: Hamiaux (2007) passim; Hamiaux et al. (2014) passim; Stewart (2016) 399–410. A sundial in the form of the prow of a warship was found on Delos; see Johnston (1985) 99–109 (#Hell. 11). An inscription from Korkyra (nO 76 = *IG* IX 12 4, 844) describes an offering from a seaman to Zeus which comprised an image of a ship; see Chaniotis and Mylonopoulos (2004) 188.

Keeping in mind the highly organized architectural system of the Tower, it is not unreasonable to conclude that the figural embellishments of the building, as well as we understand them, are likely to have functioned as parts of a unified artistic program. These include the representation of the heavens on the domed ceiling and the wind gods in flight in the sculptured frieze. The concept that unites those elements appears to be cosmic order. One has to wonder, however, how the Triton weather vane fit into this scheme. As the son of Poseidon, Triton was a maritime deity who, by blowing gently or violently into his conch shell, was able to calm or raise the waves. His actions could result in a great boon or devastating hardship for those aboard ships. One can understand why depictions of him adorned the lighthouse at Alexandria. But why would a Triton be placed atop the Tower in Athens, which is quite far inland. Is Triton here merely a marine inhabitant (like Nereids, hippocamps, and other sea monsters) who is typically related to weather, or should the reason for the weather vane in his image be reconsidered?

The argument suggested here is that the frieze depicting Boreas and his brothers evoked a specific memory along with using the wind gods as symbols of cosmic order. I propose that a major component of the artistic program of the Horologion was the defeat of the Persian fleet by the Greeks, one of the most important events in Athenian (and Greek) history. No accounts from Herodotus or others have come down to us of Triton playing a role in the battle; it is Boreas to whom the city's citizens prayed for help in destroying the Persian Navy. Thus, the figure of Triton on the roof of the Tower may simply be a reference to the maritime setting of that momentous encounter. This calls to mind the placement of Tritons on the roof of the Pergamon Altar,[123] which seem to have been intended to evoke the theme of that monument's interior frieze—Telephos' journey by sea from Greece to the homeland of his forebears in Asia Minor.

Boreas and his brothers in flight as references to victories at sea would provide the basis for there to have been a boat-shaped element in the display on or above the central floor block of the Tower. Although purely hypothetical, a number of possible reconstructions come to mind. A boat-shaped feature, as a reference to maritime victory, could have been part of a fountain, a supporting element for the water-run mechanism, or a base for a statue (a Nike?). The three columns on the south side could be seen as representing the Greek mainland or the city of Athens. The roles played by Boreas and the Athenians in the Greco-Persian Wars can be seen as significantly contributing to the preservation and propagation of Greek civilization and, thus, are equivalents to cosmic order.

A clue may be supplied by graffiti scratched into the surface of the lowest zone of the Tower's southeast interior wall.[124] The first, 1.26 meters long, is of a large ship. Many of its details are relatively clearly represented, including the rigging and oarsmen's seats,

123. Webb (1996) 65, 66.
124. Damianidis (2011) 85–99; Kienast (2014) 150–51, figs. 171 a and b.

which allow for accurate dating of the vessel to the Roman period, probably between the second and fourth centuries AD. At the lower left is the depiction of a similar but much smaller ship. Sketched beneath the two ships is a simple hunting scene with a rider and a stag. As for the significance of the images, the hunting scene cannot be connected with any suggested interpretations of the Tower's adornments. One is led to consider, however, whether the ship graffiti are also merely incidental or might have been inspired by a ship-shaped component in the display at the center of the octagonal chamber. The graffiti depictions are another curiosity in this monument rife with curiosities.

The Tower in Post-Sullan Athens

This enigmatic period, inserted between the assault on Athens by Sulla (87/86 BC) and renovations carried out by the Romans in the first century AD, is an obscure phase in the life of the monument. The meager data suggest, however, some possible answers regarding how it may have been used and what happened to the interior mechanism.

If one accepts that the Tower is listed among the entries on *IG* II^2, 1035, why and when would such an elegant and extraordinary public monument pass into private hands?

Archaeological evidence shows that structures along streets used by Sulla's army when they stormed the center of Athens suffered damage from the troops' movements, but civic and religious buildings elsewhere in the city, such as the Octagon, seem for the most part to have been spared intentional harm.[125] The relatively brief comments about the Horologion in the treatises of Vitruvius and Varro raise some questions about the building's state of preservation in the post-Sullan period, however. The authors mention the monument's architect and hometown, its octagonal form, and, most notably, the number of winds in the relief ornamentation. It is what they describe vaguely or not at all that is curious. Vitruvius states that Andronikos "caused to be made" the marble acroterion on which a bronze Triton weather vane and its accurate indicator were placed, but it is not clear if he actually saw the figure still in place on the roof or is speaking from general knowledge.[126] And while Varro refers to the monument as a horologion, it is odd that neither he nor Vitruvius (who devotes

125. Hoff (1997) 37–42.

126. "Supraque eam turrim metam marmoream perfecit et insuper Tritonem aereum conlocavit dextra manu virgam porrigentem, et ita est machinatus, uti vento circumageretur et semper contra flatum consisteret supraque imaginem flantis venti indicem virgam teneret. Itaque sunt conlocati inter solanum et austrum ab oriente hiberno eurus, ..." [And above that Tower he caused to be made a marble upright, and above it he placed a bronze Triton holding a rod in his right hand. He so contrived that it was driven round by the wind, and always faced the current of air, and held the rod as indicator above the representation of the wind blowing. Therefore there are placed between the Solanus and the Auster, the Eurus from the winter sunrising; . . . ."; trans. F. Granger].

an entire chapter to sundials and water clocks) specifically mention the sundials.[127] Thus, one must consider whether it is possible that both the bronze weather vane and the gnomons had disappeared during the Sullan attack or its aftermath and Varro was merely employing "horologion" as what may have been a commonly used term for the Octagon rather than as a description of the building's function at the time.

Equally curious is the fact that neither author comments on the mechanism within the building. Is it possible that the device was no longer in situ? Admittedly, this leads to an argument from silence, but, more important, it is an argument *about* silence.

Along with archaeological evidence for the pattern of Sullan destruction, the Tower's current relatively good state of preservation suggests that little damage was inflicted on the exterior of the building during this and other assaults on the city in the classical and Late Antique periods. Thus, the instrument inside the monument could have survived the siege. I think one should consider, however, whether the mechanism was removed subsequent to the Roman assault, thus leaving the main chamber of the Octagon empty.

During the aftermath of the sack of the city and when Sulla returned for an extended stay in 84 BC, a wide variety of valuable objects were looted from Athens. Included were statues, paintings, architectural elements from the Temple of Olympian Zeus, military shields from Athenian victories displayed in the Stoa of Zeus Eleutherius, and manuscripts from the library of Apellicon.[128] Although the device from the Tower does not appear among the items of Sullan booty in the extant historical accounts by Pliny the Elder and Pausanias, which date from the latter first century AD and the mid-second century AD, it would not be surprising if the information that has come down to us is incomplete.[129]

Evidence of Roman interest at the time in astronomical objects is illustrated by a sophisticated mechanism dating to the first half of the first century BC that was found in the remains of the Antikythera wreck, whose cargo consisted of objects being transported from Greek cities to Rome.[130] Such appropriation of scientific instruments by Romans is documented as early as 211 BC; among the objects looted by Marcellus and taken to Rome after the siege of Syracuse were the two celestial globes fabricated by Archimedes, which were discussed above.[131] The lesser of the two spheres was retained by Marcellus in his personal collection. The more impressive globe was installed in the

127. Vitruvius Bk. 9.8. The fact that Vitruvius did not mention the sundials led the distinguished French mathematician and astronomer Delambre to conclude incorrectly that they were made at some time after the completion of the Tower; see Stuart and Revett (1825) 37 *n. b.*

128. Pliny *NH* Bk. 36.45; Pausanias Bk. 10.21.3; see also Hoff (1997) 37, 41, 43.

129. As previously quoted in the Preface, Haselberger (2014) 36, while taking into consideration an argument *ex silentio* regarding the great horologium in Rome, points out: "The Horologium of Augustus, with its extraordinary timepiece, was a major monument of Augustan propaganda.... The silence of Augustan-era sources is hardly an argument against its significance; even Augustus himself 'omits' the Horologium (as well as his Mausoleum) in his formal account of achievements."

130. Freeth and Jones (2012) passim; *The Antikythera Mechanism Research Project* website.

131. Cicero, *De Republica,* 1.21–22; Miles (2008) 61–65.

Temple of Virtue.[132] That the mechanism within the Tower may have been a tempting prize to the Roman general or one of his cohorts certainly fits this pattern of acquisition.

Thus, if the interior of the Horologion had been looted in the years immediately after the siege by Sulla, leaving the chamber empty and elements on the exterior of the building—the bronze Triton and the gnomons—missing, the Tower would no longer be able to carry out its original functions. The acanthus finial atop the roof does show evidence of damage, the upper half having been broken off and then later repaired. Kienast attributes the injury to pressure over time from the weight of the Triton.[133] It is also possible, however, that the damage resulted from the weather vane having been roughly removed when being looted. Even though one cannot be certain about the fate of the Tower's interior mechanism, I suggest it was at this time and under these circumstances that the water-powered apparatus was removed. The Clepsydra springhouse on the north slope of the Acropolis, which likely furnished the water for the Horologion, was severely damaged in the Sullan siege; consequently, it was unlikely to have been able to supply water to the Tower during this period.[134]

With the mechanism gone, the Tower would have been little more than a large empty chamber. Whoever leased it would have had limited options for its use. Inadequate lighting may have made it difficult for the space to serve as a shop or workshop, so the large empty room would probably have best served as a kind of storehouse.[135] In that case, its doors probably would have been closed and locked much of the time. Consequently, the building would not have housed a water-run device or a cult; it would have looked to ancient visitors much as it looks to the visitor today.

A curious passage in M. Cetius Faventinus' *Artis architectonicae priuatis usibus adbreuiatus liber* (2.2–3) suggests an intriguing possibility regarding the fate of the Triton weather vane and the water-run device. Cetius wrote this abridged version of Vitruvius' *De Architectura* around the end of the third century. To the Vitruvian discussion of the Horologion in Athens and its reliefs of eight winds, Cetius adds this comment:

> Sed plerique duodecim ventos esse adseverant, ut est in urbe Roma Triton aeneus cum totidem thoracibus ventorum factus ad exemplum Andronici Cyrrestis.[136]
>
> But most men assert that there are twelve winds, exemplified at Rome by the bronze Triton above twelve winds, of whom only the heads and upper torsos are depicted, on a structure made after the prototype of Andronicus Cyrrhestes (trans. P. Webb).

132. The third and second centuries BC had also seen the first sundials set up in Rome—by L. Papirius Cursor near the Temple of Quirinus in 292 BC, by M. Valerius Messalla, near the Rostra in 262 BC, and by Q. Marcius Philippus near the Rostra in 164 BC.

133. Kienast (2014) 149.

134. Parsons (1943) 239–41; Hoff (1997) 40–42.

135. In a possible case of history repeating itself, the Tower served as a storage facility for the Greek Archaeological Society from 1837–1846.

136. Cam (2001) 6–7. Another example depicting twelve winds is found on a dodecagonal base (in the Vatican collections), which is inscribed with the name of a wind on each of its twelve sides (*IG* XIV 1308); it was found near San Pietro in Vincoli in 1779; see Plommer (1973) 89. See also note 3, above.

Thus, some type of construction inspired by the Athenian Octagon was built in Rome but displayed twelve winds instead of eight. There is no clue as to where this monument, which has not survived, stood or when it was built, although it likely was after Vitruvius published his books in the early Augustan period, since he does not include it in his commentary. Cetius does not describe the size of the Roman structure, but one cannot help wondering whether it was large enough to have been crowned by Andronikos' Triton and to have housed the Athenian instrument.

The Roman Renovations

In the early imperial period, the neighborhood of the Horologion would have been a very busy place. In the immediate vicinity the great Roman Agora lay to the west. A large public latrine stood to the northwest, and, as discussed above, to the southeast were two long rectangular buildings—the so-called Agoranomion and the enclosed Hellenistic stoa. The Octagon would have been accessible to the sizable crowds that were living, working, and shopping in the area.

The renovations and restorations implemented by the Romans in the period after the Tower was reclaimed as a public monument can be documented primarily for the interior, which provides evidence that the water system was restored. It is not unreasonable to assume, however, that if the bronze weather vane and the gnomons had been damaged or removed in the first century BC, they also would have been replaced as part of the Roman rehabilitation of the monument.

By the time repairs were carried out in the first century AD, water seems no longer to have entered into and flowed through the Octagon in underground pipes. Instead, water appears to have been brought to the building via an aqueduct laid atop the arched façade of the building complex to the southeast and from there connected to the south side of the Tower.[137] A low door was opened in the common wall between the annex and the main room, providing access from within the building for maintenance of the system. A carved ornamental frame is extant on the left side and at the top left corner of the door; no frame remains on the right side because of missing and damaged blocks,[138] breakage that most likely occurred during one of several military sieges of the city in Late Antiquity. Instead of water flowing from the annex through the underground channel to the main room, a groove was carved into the surface of the floor into which a new aboveground water pipe was laid between the square drain in the annex and the central aperture in the octagonal chamber (Ills. 32, 33).

The relative positions of the various holes and grooves in the floor help clarify the chronological sequence of their implementation. In review, elements identified previously as dating to the Hellenistic period include in the main chamber the central

137. Kienast (2014) 29–31.
138. Kienast (2014) fig. 168.

aperture, beddings for three columns, and two series of small round holes; and in the annex the square drain, the inflow hole, and the channel for a pipe above the inflow. The central aperture, the central column bedding, and the annex drain each lie directly on the north-south axis.

Dating to the Roman renovations, a rough and somewhat irregular channel (0.10 meters wide and 0.06 meters deep) for an aboveground water pipe extending from the annex drain to the center of the main chamber lies flat within the floor with no decline toward either end. Its depth would likely have resulted in the pipe being scarcely visible. The conduit does not lie on a straight line between the annex and the main chamber. Before exiting the low doorway, it makes a jog so it can pass to the east of the central column, indicating that the column was still in place and was intended to remain in place. The conduit then bends slightly and trifurcates into grooves that connect at the southeast border of the central aperture and with the beddings for the lateral columns. The marble pavement around the column bedding on the east side has heavy water stains.[139] The kind of device powered by water flowing through the pipe in this channel during the Roman period remains open to question. That a water-run instrument was reinstalled in the Horologion is evident.

It can be argued that with the restoration of the building came the restoration of its cultic and commemorative attributes. As Shear describes it, during the reign of Augustus there was a "well documented program to restore the sanctuaries and *temene* of the gods and heroes, which had been damaged in the wars of the Hellenistic period or had fallen into disrepair over the course of time."[140] In Alcock's survey of Athens in the early imperial period, she too finds that the Romans' attention was placed on existing monuments rather than on newly built memorials. A "lack of monumentalization should not, however, be confused with a lack of regard. . . . [L]iterary or epigraphic evidence does not speak of *new* monuments, but certainly attests to commemorative rituals at old or renewed ones."[141] In relation to these memorial structures, Alcock finds a pervasive interest in the expression of reverence for the Greco-Persian Wars. An important reminder of the glory of classical Greece, this theme was also viewed by Rome as a metaphor for its conflict with the Parthians. The role played by Boreas and the other wind gods in victory over the Persians may not have been the only impetus for the restoration of the Tower, but it was an important story for both the Athenians and the Romans, and it is certainly reasonable to consider that it would have contributed to the desire to return the building to its original state.

139. Kienast (2014) 40. Noble and Price (1968) 348, 353, hypothesize that the channel held a pipe that may have supplied water for decorative fountains (at either side of a water clock) in the original Hellenistic building.

140. Shear (1981) 357–59, 365 and nn. 2–9.

141. Alcock (2002) 77–82.

II

THE CHRISTIAN TOWER

Athens in Late Antiquity

Transformation from a Pagan to a Christian City

Arriving at an understanding of the condition of the Octagon during the time span between the first century AD (after Roman renovations) and the Tower's conversion to Christian use is a challenging task. Restoration of the piping system is evidence that the water-run device—an orrery or other apparatus—was reinstalled during the Roman repairs. We do not know, however, how long the instrument remained in place and was functioning. The building's size and singular architecture are indications that the mechanism would have been large and complex, probably requiring a certain amount of maintenance and repair. Thus, it is conceivable that over several centuries the device ceased to function or did not survive one of the various military sieges.

The Herulian invasion of AD 267 and the raids by Alaric and the Visigoths in AD 395/6 certainly caused significant damage to Athens.[1] In the Herulian siege, public monuments and private houses throughout the city were destroyed. The Greek Agora was devastated. On its west and north sides, the Temple of Apollo Patroös and three stoas were left standing, but important buildings such as the Bouleuterion and the Metroön were gone. Structures in the central and southern sections completely vanished, leaving what seems to have been an open area that after a time was simply covered by vegetation. The great Stoa of Attalos and other monuments on the east side were in a ruinous state.

A number of buildings in the immediate area of the Tower survived the attack in serviceable condition. These include the so-called Agoranomion, the southern sector of the Roman Agora and its two entrance gates, and the eastern rooms and southeastern peristyle of the so-called Library of Hadrian. Because of the location of the Horologion near other structures that remained intact, it can be assumed that it sustained no debilitating damage. This district, along with the Acropolis, was enclosed in a defense fortification—the Post-Herulian Wall—that was constructed out of *spolia*

1. Frantz (1965) 187–200; Frantz (1988) 3–14, 48–70, 117–22; Castrén (1994) 1–14; Castrén (1999) 211–23.

opima recovered from the many ruined buildings in and around Athens (Ill. 1).[2] Consequently, the active city center was now reduced to an area of approximately forty acres north of the Acropolis and east of the Greek Agora.

In the century following the Herulian invasion, even with such widespread and severe destruction, Athens gradually recovered and became relatively stable economically and culturally throughout much of Late Antiquity. By the fourth century, the city had regained its prominence as a seat of higher education, attracting numerous students from all areas of the Byzantine world. Among them were the future Roman emperor Julian and the Cappadocian Fathers, Basil the Great and Gregory of Nazianzus, both of whom lived in Athens for a number of years when they studied under the renowned rhetorician Himerios.[3] By the beginning of the fifth century, subsequent to the sack by Alaric and the Visigoths, Athens saw something of a construction boom, including new buildings in the Greek Agora.

Few artifacts from Athens dating to the early Christian period have been identified, and the history of that community at the time is not well understood. The Athenian church did send a representative (Bishop Pistos) to the church-changing Council of Nicaea in AD 325, but he was one of only three bishops from Greece to join the congregation of approximately two hundred members from the eastern provinces. The transition from polytheism to Christianity seems to have been a delayed process here, and pagans and Christians lived their different lifestyles side by side, even burying their dead in the same cemeteries. As Frantz describes the situation, "it would, indeed, be hard to find [another] place where the inhabitants were so unreceptive to Christianity."[4] Unlike many cities in the Byzantine Empire, Athens retained its classical name, and certain pagan institutions continued—the Council of the Areopagus until the close of the fourth century, the Panathenaic Procession (including hauling the ritual ship up to the Acropolis) into the fifth century, and the Archonship until the last quarter of the fifth century.[5] Even though the Code of Theodosius, issued in AD 435, was intended to bring the practice of polytheistic cults to an end, this and other similar decrees seem to have been widely ignored in Athens.[6] A clause in the code giving authority for implementation of the law to local magistrates[7] meant that in Athens decisions regarding when and how to carry out these dictates were in the purview of pagan officials, men who were greatly influenced by the Neoplatonic Academy.

The Christian community did continue to grow and become more economically prosperous throughout the fifth century, however, and political power began to shift.

2. Thompson (1959) 61–72.
3. Basil resided in Athens for six years; Gregory for a decade, from AD 348–358.
4. Frantz (1965) 188. A similar process of late Christianization, as well as tolerance of pagans and Christians living and practicing their religions side by side, has been documented for many cities in the Peloponnese; see Saradi-Mendelovici (1990) 47–61; Sweetman (2015) passim.
5. *IG* II^2, 3818.
6. Sixteen decrees referring to pagan cults were issued in the century before the Theodosian Code. Their focus, however, was on sacrifice, not on temples and their furnishings; see Frantz (1988) 69.
7. *Code Theod.* 16.10.25.

In AD 529, Justinian contributed significantly to the demise of classical culture in Athens when he ordered the Platonic school closed, causing most philosophers and students to move to other centers of learning.

Athens suffered its most devastating siege in the 580s when the Slavs and Avars invaded, ravaging Attica and causing much ruination in the city. The economically viable still-pagan city of the fifth century was reduced to a place of dismay and decrepitude at the end of the sixth century. In the vicinity of the Horologion, the first known Christian church built in Athens, a fifth-century tetraconch structure located in the courtyard of the nearby Library of Hadrian, was destroyed.[8] This may be the period during which damage to the Tower's access door between the main chamber and the annex occurred and when any classical apparatus, including water tanks and pipes, if still in place, vanished.

There is little evidence of major building activity during the following few centuries. Athens, which had been the most important university city in the classical world, was no longer a major pagan cultural and educational center but instead had become—by comparison—a modest Christian town.

Date of the Conversion of the Tower to Christian Use

Compared to many structures in the center of the now much reduced in size city north of the Acropolis, the Tower in Late Antiquity was still a solidly constructed building in relatively good condition. More so than other classical monuments that were converted to Christian use (see Appendix 2), its sculpture and architecture would have been adapted fairly easily. The male figures adorning the exterior would have been viewed not as pagan wind gods but instead as personifications of natural forces, an expression of a larger movement in this period of allegorizing classical myth in order to create a distinctive science that combined classical and biblical world views. The ways in which Christian representations of the winds continued the categories of Graeco-Roman cosmology is perhaps best seen in the sixth-century book on astronomy and natural history, *De Rerum Natura,* by Spanish theologian and scholar Isidore of Seville, who appears to have drawn on Suetonius' *De Natura Rerum* (not extant).[9] Even the inscribed identifications on the Tower would have been familiar to educated Christians, for both Greek and Latin names of the winds remained in use in both literature and scientific texts.[10]

Exactly when the cult of the winds was brought to an end is unclear. By the second quarter of the fifth century, the Imperial cult seems to have ceased being practiced in the Library of Hadrian when the tetraconch church was built in its courtyard (see

8. See Appendix 1.

9. Seznec (1953) 3, 14–17, 41–43; Obrist (1997) passim.

10. It is possible some viewers may have interpreted the winged figures as angels. The eighteenth century English poet John Dalton believed that Raphael based his representation of God in his "Creation of the World" on one of the Tower's wind gods (most likely Boreas); see Dalton (1752) 20–21.

Appendix 1). There are various possibilities as to how the Tower could have continued to function at that time: the cult may have persisted for an unspecified period; the cult may have been discontinued, with the building serving purely as a civic structure; the building may have been closed for an indeterminate period; or the building could have been converted to Christian use when the tetraconch building was erected. In whatever manner the Octagon functioned in the fifth and sixth centuries, however, its status irrevocably changed as Athens changed from pagan to Christian.

Along with the fact that the renowned tetraconch church had been built nearby, the Christianization of Late Antique Athens in the area of the Horologion is supported by the conversion during this period of the mid-first-century AD "Agoranomion" southeast of the Tower. The "Agoranomion" has several Christian symbols carved into its walls, leading Orlandos and others to conclude that it was reconfigured as a church. Frantz, moreover, believes that the "Agoranomion" was one of the first ancient buildings in Athens to be used as a church (see Appendix 2). Further evidence of a Christian presence is the existence of Christian graves in the area outside the Tower's northeast porch whose stelai are dated on the basis of their carving style to between the fifth and seventh centuries.[11]

The damage and upheaval caused to Athens by the Slav and Avar invasion at the close of the sixth century left the city in ruins, with the economy shattered and no resources for new construction. It is likely that the well-built and relatively intact Tower was called into Christian service in the following decades. The consecration of the Horologion is indicated first by crosses carved into its exterior and interior surfaces.[12] Two crosses, each inscribed within a circle and described anachronistically as "Maltese" because of their structure, are etched into the jambs of the northwest door at 2.73 meters above floor level. Frantz finds them similar to those on the Christian Temple of Hephaestus, which was converted into a church in the seventh century (see Appendix 2). A third Christian symbol—a Latin cross (0.12 meters high and 0.065 meters wide)—is incised into the lowest zone of the east interior wall beneath the first cornice, about 1.35 meters above floor level (Ill. 34). Two crosses of similar size, form, and workmanship are carved into the third course of the north exterior wall and the fourth course of the west exterior wall. The presence of these images would have been dictated by the Theodosian Code, which, when pagan temples and shrines were to be transformed into Christian buildings, required their walls to be purified by the sign of the cross, a practice known as *sphragis*.[13] As described by Kiilerich, this was a way "of

11. Orlandos (1964) 58–59; Travlos (1971) 37; Frantz (1988) 68–73. While Christian tombs on the north slope of the Areopagus are tentatively dated to the fifth century, the earliest precisely dated chronological evidence for Christian burials within the city walls are two gold coins of AD 578–582 from a grave on the south slope of the Acropolis below the Parthenon; see Castrén (1999) 221–22 and n. 44.

12. Orlandos (1964) 59, #136, fig. 112; Noble and Price (1968) 348 n. 14; Travlos (1971) fig. 376; von Freeden (1983) 17 and n. 79; Frantz (1988) 71–72 and n. 101; Kienast (2014) 149 and n. 550, 152; figs. 170 and 175; pl. 31a.

13. *Cod. Theod.* XVI. 10. 25.

neutralizing and of, so to speak, baptizing the object. By placing one or more crosses on or near a pagan object, potential evil forces lose their power."[14]

Further compelling evidence for conversion of the Tower is offered by Byzantine paintings whose fragmentary remains have been uncovered from beneath limestone stucco applied to the interior walls during renovation of the structure by Sufi Muslim dervishes in the eighteenth century. In the upper region of Zone 3 are the remains of an angel, and between the doors is a saint on horseback (Ill. 35). As described by members of the Greek restoration team in 2015, "work associated with the conservation and consolidation of the Horologeion of Andronikos Kyrristos, the so-called 'Tower of the Winds' in the Roman Agora, has identified the remains of Byzantine wall-paintings previously disguised beneath Late Ottoman plasterwork. Neither the exact theme nor the date of the painting is currently clear, though it is probably to be associated with the Early Byzantine conversion of the Horologeion, evidenced by the incision of crosses across the structure and the presence of Christian burials beyond the north-eastern entrance."[15] Other members of the team date the paintings to the thirteenth or fourteenth centuries.[16]

Renovations Made during the Christian Conversion

Few changes were required to convert the Tower from a pagan to a Christian monument. Other than incising the crosses and applying the paintings, there is evidence of this process in alterations to the floor of the main chamber. Eight curved grooves of varying lengths (0.10 meters wide by 0.50 meters deep and ca. 0.83–0.90 meters long) provided anchoring for a balustrade encircling the central aperture at the same distance and lying along an arc with the three columns, circumscribing an area 2.96 meters in diameter. A ninth, parallel to the groove on the east side, is likely to have been an error made by the stonemason, as is another (only a few centimeters long) on the northeast side. The balustrade can be seen to have made accommodation for the columns in that the four grooves on the south side of the room abut and/or lie between the column beddings instead of extending into or over them. Where the barrier was not interrupted by the columns, the grooves are separated from one another by spaces approximately 0.12 meters wide (Ills. 18, 36).[17]

Large fragments of this marble latticed balustrade (Ill. 37) were recovered by Stuart and Revett from meters-deep fill excavated from beneath a wooden floor that had been installed in the Octagon by the Sufi dervishes. Others were found outside in the vicinity of the Tower and in the area of the Roman Agora. The extant segments are

14. Kiilerich (2005) 99–106, esp. 102.
15. Smith (2015) 25, fig. 35.
16. The limestone was removed from the interior walls during recent conservation of the monument; see: http://efaathculture.gr/wp/content/uploads/2016/05/the-conservation-and-valorization-of-the-horologon-of-andronikos-of-kyrrhos.
17. Kienast (2014) 38, 41, pl. 3.

reconstructed to elbow height, approximately 0.90 meters. Along the upper edge is a half-round molding. Along the bottom is a projecting element that fits into the floor groove. The latticed panels are longer than the projecting element and thus bridged the gaps between the curved grooves.[18]

Unfortunately, the lozenge- or diamond-shape motif of the balustrade's panels is of little use in determining its date, for this pattern can be found over a broad period of time. Examples include the second-storey parapet of the mid-second century BC Stoa of Attalos in the Greek Agora and a seventh century AD altar screen from a church on the Cycladic island Sikinos.[19] Orlandos and Kienast, among most scholars, consider the barrier to be original to the Hellenistic Octagon where, they believe, it would have protected the water-operated mechanism from visitors and may even have been connected to the functioning of the apparatus.[20]

Two factors, however, provide strong indication that the balustrade was not part of the Hellenistic (or Roman) monument, but was a Christian addition. The first is related to the organization of its installation. The curved grooves do not align with the eight sides of the building; the grooves are instead somewhat haphazardly placed with little relationship to the octagonal plan. This lack of axial alignment contradicts the design and execution standards of the Hellenistic architect.

Second, the fact that large fragments of the Tower's balustrade were found buried in the fill inside the building during the eighteenth-century excavations is evidence that it was in place and in use through the end of the last period in which the marble floor was still exposed—that is, throughout the Christian phase, which covers a period of more than a millennium. This conclusion is supported by the account of the Turkish traveler Evliya, who after entering the Octagon in 1668 stated that the building contained a grave, the casket was in place, its chronogram was visible, and Christians still visited the monument on the saint's feast day.[21] Thus, one can construe from his comments that the Christian cult was active and that the floor was not buried beneath meters of debris.

No other interior features were extant by the time Stuart and Revett cleared the interior of the building. It seems probable that the water-run mechanism and the piping system did not survive the centuries between their reinstallation by the Romans and the end of Late Antiquity, especially after the destruction wrought by the Slavs and Avars. The columns survived for a certain amount of time, for they were clearly originally integrated into the circle of the balustrade. But they too disappeared at some point over the centuries, as no fragments were found by Stuart and Revett. Therefore,

18. Orlandos (1919) 15–16, fig. 2; Noble and Price (1968) 347–48, pl. 116, fig. 16; Kienast (2014) 38–39, figs. 50–53.

19. Stoa of Attalos: Travlos (1971) 505, fig. 645; Lawrence (1996) fig. 344. Sikinos: Frantz et al. (1969) 418, fig. 3, pl. 104.33. The lozenge motif on the balustrade from the Tower is open-work. The parapet of the reconstructed Stoa of Attalos (a faithful replica of the Hellenistic original) and the altar screen are carved in relief; the background of the stoa relief, however, was painted blue in order to create the impression that it was open-work.

20. Kienast (2014) 38–39, and nn. 161 and 163.

21. MacKay (1969) 468–69; Dankoff and Kim (2010) 289.

since all other interior features that can be dated to the Hellenistic and Roman periods were no longer extant when the Dilettanti excavated, it seems highly unlikely that the balustrade was the only original element to have remained in place for seventeen centuries. This and its comparatively crude installation make it more likely that it was a later addition.

Baptistery, Church, or Martyrium?

Determining specifically how the Christianized Tower functioned in Byzantine Athens—as a baptistery, a church, or a martyrium—is complicated by the fact that these structures were closely linked architecturally. Many of the buildings in each of the three categories were, like the Tower, centralized structures—circular, square, cruciform, or octagonal. Baptisteries and martyria shared other elements as well, because death, burial, and resurrection were central to both; martyrs, after all, were believed to have been baptized in their own blood. There are incidences of baptisteries that were built above martyria, baptisteries that were converted into martyria, and martyria that were converted into baptisteries.[22] Exploring in turn the possibilities that the Octagon served as a baptistery, a church, or a martyrium will facilitate examination of the features that were present in the building during the period of its Christian occupation.

The octagonal floor plan in Christian architecture was a symbolic reference to the eighth day, the day of Christ's resurrection and the renewal of creation.[23] It is used for each of the three types of Christian buildings mentioned above, although it seems particularly relatable to baptisteries where it evokes the rituals performed there. Orlandos was the first to propose that the Horologion was converted for use as a baptistery. Frantz subsequently suggested that the church served by the Octagon would have been located in the adjacent "Agoranomion".[24] The Tower initially appears to be well suited to such a purpose, since the building was constructed to have access to water. No argument can be made, however, that the piping systems—from the source of water at the Clepsydra spring to the Tower and within the building—survived Late Antiquity.

Small also supports Orlandos' idea, proposing that the inner series of small holes in the floor anchored slender columns that encircled the balustrade, inside of which stood a baptismal font (*fons vitae*). Resting on the colonnade, he suggests, would have been a canopy (*tegurium*).[25] In such a reconstruction, however, the three Hellenistic columns would have stood side by side with three of the slender columns, the hole for one of which nearly abuts the bedding of the large column on the southwest (Ill. 33).

22. Tsafrir (1993) 1–16; Jensen (2011) 234–43; Ferguson (2009) 417–19, 669–70.
23. Jensen (2011) 244–47; she also discusses here the significance of the number eight in Greek and Roman numerology. See also Underwood (1950) 43–138, esp. 81–87; Meer (1961) 379–82; Koch (1996) 14–15, 34–39; Ferguson (2009) 759 and n. 5, 819.
24. Orlandos (1964) 58–59. Frantz (1988) 71, places the conversion of the "Agoranomion" into a church prior to the conversion of the Octagon into a baptistery.
25. Small (1980) passim.

It is clear that the three Hellenistic columns were retained in place at the time of the building's conversion, because the bedding grooves of the balustrade do not extend into the footings for the columns but instead accommodate them. It is highly unlikely that smaller and larger columns would have been positioned in this manner. If it were desired to leave the large columns in place, it would have been a simple matter either to rotate the placement of eight smaller columns or to move them farther out from the larger columns and the balustrade. Small's reconstruction also includes fifteen slender columns anchored in the holes around the perimeter of the chamber that would have articulated the walls and supported a second higher canopy. This reconstruction is highly improbable, for the outer canopy would have obscured the building's high-domed ceiling, a desired element in a Christian building.[26]

Along with the problems associated with Small's suggested reconstruction, other difficulties exist in viewing the Octagon as a baptistery. First, baptisteries in Greece in the early Byzantine period generally consisted of at least two rooms, one of which would be a changing room.[27] The Tower could not easily accommodate space for changing beyond a curtain being hung from the three columns on the south side of the chamber. The annex would have been large enough if the shelf had been removed, but that was not done. Second, the balustrade would have entirely encircled and enclosed the area in which a *fons vitae* would have stood, allowing no access for officiants and initiates. Third, the rare reports of the Christianized Tower in the historical record (to be discussed below) refer to the monument as a church or, in one instance, describe the burial of a saint within the building. It is never defined as a baptistery.

Among early churches are a number that were octagonal, the most famous of which was the so-called Golden Octagon, built in Antioch by Constantine ca. AD 327 (destroyed ca. AD 527). But the classification of the Tower as a church results in one of the difficulties encountered when identifying it as a baptistery. The balustrade, which in a church would have served as a chancel barrier (*templon*), would have entirely enclosed the area around the altar, prohibiting access by priests. Another problem exists as well. Athenians converted few classical monuments into churches (see Appendices 1 and 2). Most of those that were converted had been pagan temples whose orientation lay on an east-west axis, which could relatively easily be reversed so that an altar could be placed in an apse on the east end of the building.[28] The north-south axis of the Tower would have presented significant difficulty in reconfiguring the monument as a church.

The evidence more strongly suggests that the function of the Tower when converted in early Byzantine Athens to Christian use was as a commemorative church, or "memoria martyrum". *Loca sancta,* or τόποι ἅγιοι, were an invention of the fourth

26. Jensen (2011) 238.
27. Ferguson (2009) 832; Volanakis (1976) 139–40.
28. While not all churches lay on a strict west-east axis, it was generally the case. Early churches in northern Greece have been shown consistently to have had a slight southeast orientation, but they did not express an extreme deviation from the west-east axis; see Iliades (2006) passim.

century.[29] Martyr cults were important to Christian communities, and pilgrims often traveled long distances to visit renowned religious sites. The establishment of a cult brought revenue, honor, and prestige to the martyr's family, village, city, or region.[30] In this way, martyrs and martyria were similar to Greek heroes and heroa. The bones of a saint held supernatural power that could provide "cures, protection from oppression, help in finding lost objects, assistance in settling disputes"[31], and in other areas of greater and lesser importance to the lives of individuals and the community. "*Praesentia,* the physical presence of the holy, whether in the midst of a particular community or in the possession of particular individuals, was the greatest blessing that a late-antique Christian could enjoy."[32]

Most martyria were centralized buildings with high domes emphasizing their midpoint, an architectural form inspired by monumental Roman mausolea.[33] The Octagon shares these characteristics. While the structure and siting of martyria varied, they were frequently located near the entrance to a church.[34] This lends credence to the hypothesis that the "Agoranomion" and the Tower may have been united as an ecclesiastical complex.

By the sixth or seventh centuries nearly all church altars contained saints' relics, resulting in the virtual elimination of the distinction between extra-urban and urban burials, and interment near a martyr's tomb (*depositio ad sanctos*) was a widespread practice in all geographic regions.[35] Christian gravestones found in close proximity to the Tower, dating to between the fifth and seventh centuries,[36] thus lend support to the premise that the building held the relics of a saint.[37]

29. Yasin (2009) 26.
30. Limberis (2011) passim.
31. Geary (1986) 175–76.
32. Brown (1981) 89–96.
33. Tsafrir (1993) 5–6. Tall centralized martyria were common, but martyria did take a variety of forms, such as basilicas, small chapels, modest rooms, and stone tables in the open air for feasts of the dead (*mensae*).
34. Yasin (2009) 156, 161.
35. Brown (1981) 5, 34–35, 69–71. For the importance of Christian burial within city walls, see Limberis (2005) passim. The practice of interring saints' bones in or under altars was finally written into canonical law at the Second Council of Nicaea in AD 787. See: Braun (1924) vol. 1, 525–661; Grig (2004) 87; Yasin (2009) 152–54.
36. Meer (1961) 492–94; Frantz (1988) 72.
37. Saints Basil the Great and Gregory of Nazianzus lived in Athens for a number of years in the mid-fourth century. During their lives they were unflagging in their promotion of the cults of martyrs, which they believed were of vital importance to the sanctification of cities. Despite their affection for Athens and its local churches, however, there is no evidence that either Basil or Gregory facilitated the donation of relics to the city. See Brown (1981) 94; McGuckin (2001) vii, 74–76; Bitton-Ashkelony (2005) 30–44.

Excavations at Kenchreai, east of Corinth, carried out in 2009, uncovered the remains of a monumental octagonal structure (14.25 m interior diameter) dating to the early fifth century AD. The entrance is in the north wall; a series of piers separates the center of the chamber from an ambulatory. Seven cist graves were found near the building and aligned with its walls. The excavators conclude the monument had a funerary function, although they have not yet determined whether as a martyrium or for the burial of a local wealthy resident; see Morgan (2009–2010) 22–23.

As a martyrium, there would not have been many visitors entering the Octagon on a regular basis other than on the saint's feast day; thus, the monument's two doors may have been closed and possibly locked much of the time. Three small holes outside the threshold of the northeast door are evidence that at some point a small single-leaf door (0.70 meters wide) was installed (Ills. 8c, 36).[38] While a date for this occurrence has not been determined, it is possible that the narrow door was inserted when the building was converted, as it would have been considered sufficient to handle the much diminished traffic.

Stuart and Revett reported no remains of a casket or reliquary in their excavations. They did recover several human bones, however, from the fill inside the building below the first cornice, which they assumed to be evidence of a Christian burial.[39] As mentioned above, a burial within the Octagon is described by the Turkish traveler Evliya Çelebi, who visited Athens in the century prior to Stuart and Revett. In his account of the Tower, which appears in his *Book of Travels* (*Seyahatname*), he states: "Inside this pavilion-shaped dome there is a tomb in which all the Christian infidels believe that Philip the Greek is buried, and on their infamous feast days they visit it. At the head and the foot of this grave a chronogram [one assumes of the martyr's death[40]] has been written in the Greek language."[41] The marble balustrade would have enclosed the area where the small casket or reliquary stood.

A number of early Byzantine reliquaries found in situ in churches in Syria may offer examples regarding the size and form of casket that could have been placed within the Tower. The most common type is a small sarcophagus capped by a gabled lid with acroteria at the corners; they measure ca. 1.00–1.50 meters long and 0.50–0.70 meters high. Channels are drilled in the lids and bases, through which a liquid (presumably olive oil) would be poured and then collected after coming in contact with the relics. Since worshippers would be blessed and sanctified through touching a tomb, the placement of the casket in the Octagon near the balustrade may have permitted them to do so. In order to receive a blessing, however, it was not absolutely necessary that pilgrims touch a relics' container with their hand. Optic theory in Late Antiquity defined sight as a superior form of touch; it was believed that actual rays emanated from the eyes, made contact with an object, and then returned through the eyes, imprinting the image on the brain.[42]

38. Kienast (2014) 151.
39. Stuart and Revett (1762) 18; Stuart and Revett (1825) 43.
40. A letter written by Cyprian, Bishop of Carthage (*Ep.* 12.2.1), in the mid-third century emphasizes the importance of keeping records of the names and dates of the deaths of martyrs. The day of the saint's death is described as his/her birthday into everlasting life (*dies natalis*). The death dates of the Apostles had been known from the time they were martyred.
41. MacKay (1969) 468–69; Dankoff and Kim (2010) 289.
42. Maraval (2002) 72–73; Frank (2000a) passim, esp. 104–33; Frank (2000b) 98–115; Yasin (2009) 165–68, fig. 4.9; Limberis (2011) 60.

Evliya Çelebi and the Identity of the Martyr as the Apostle Philip

Greece (in general) and Athens (in particular) are rarely mentioned by ancient or modern authors in connection with martyrs from the early Christian and early Byzantine periods. The Orthodox community was small during those centuries because the city came to Christianity late; thus, there was a paucity of candidates for martyrdom. Among the few documented are the Apostle Andrew, who is believed to have been crucified and buried in the northwestern Peloponnese at Patras in AD 60, and Publius, an early bishop of Athens who was martyred ca. AD 125.[43] It is not known, however, whether local cults were established in their honor. The only evidence (disputed by some scholars) of an early Christian cult in Athens is that of Saint Leonidas.[44] A large three-aisled basilica on the outskirts of the city on an islet in the Ilissus River was built in the first half of the fifth century on the site of an earlier building. A door in its north wall connected to a domed cruciform martyrium for this bishop of Athens, who died in AD 250. Clearly, in Late Antiquity there appears to have been a dearth of saints' relics in Athens.[45]

So, who is the person said to be interred in the Tower and identified by Evliya simply as Philip the Greek? Evliya's descriptions of this and other ancient monuments, as well as his concept of Athenian history, are often a mixture of reality and fancy. He describes the accuracy of the Octagon's sundials,[46] but his commentary is not free from error. For example, he characterizes the beardless winds as female. Therefore, how reliable is his information about the burial within the building?

Evliya (1611–ca. 1684) was an Ottoman courtier who came from a wealthy family with close ties to the imperial government in Istanbul. His father was the chief goldsmith for the sultan, and his uncle was a Grand Vizier. Evliya was a pious man, educated in a madrassa, who had comprehensive knowledge of Persian and Arabic culture. But as a young man he also learned to read Greek and Latin from a non-Muslim named Simyon who was employed in his father's workshop.[47] Evliya was one

43. Andrew's bones were sent to Constantinople in the mid-third century; Delehaye (1933) 227.

44. Grabar (1946)vol. 1, 107, 109, 336, fig. 43; Chatzidakis (1960) 2–3, figs. 7–12; Korres, et al. (2003) 200, figs. 6 and 7; Kaldellis (2009) 170–71 and nn. 8–10. The hagiographies of the bishop of Athens and Saint Leonidas of Corinth appear to have been comingled in later centuries; see Limberis (2005) 450–52 and n. 38.

45. In the early and middle Byzantine periods, Constantinople (the "New Jerusalem" / "New Rome") acquired the most extensive collection of relics in the Empire. Even so, that city had few local martyrs before the mid-fourth century. Evidence suggests that only Saint Acacius was the object of a martyr cult at the time of the consecration of Constantinople on May 11, 330. See Wortley (2009a) passim, esp. 355–56, 371–73, 378; Wortley (2009b) passim, esp. 487, 490–92, 494–95.

46. Evliya seems to be evaluating the sun dials solely on the basis of the carved lines in the marble walls; he makes no mention of gnomons. He refers to the designer as a great master, but it is not clear he knows to what time period the astronomer belongs; see Dankoff and Kim (2010) 290.

47. Pallis (1951) passim, esp. 56–63; Dankoff (1989) 29; Dankoff, et al. (2004) 27; Dankoff and Kim (2010) xii-xvii.

of the most widely traveled persons of his time, visiting almost every area of the Ottoman Empire and lands beyond its borders. The ten-volume *Seyahatname* (published ca. 1680) has been broadly recognized as a valuable resource for the period in regard to a wide variety of data, such as size of populations, ethnic representations in population groups, and descriptions of paintings, sculptures, urban landscapes (including civic and religious structures), and local dress and behaviors.[48] While it is agreed that details in his accounts of Ottoman and Islamic architecture and furnishings are precise and systematic, his treatment of classical and Christian monuments admittedly can be less exact.[49]

Evliya's information about the founding of Athens and the lives of renowned historical persons from ancient Greece is derived predominantly from the literature of myths and legends.[50] He believes that the Greeks were descended from the dynasty of King David; that Athens was established by King Solomon, who flew there from Jerusalem on the wind; and that the city later was expanded and embellished by Philip II and Alexander the Great, who were fifth- and sixth-generation descendants of Solomon. Even though Evliya expresses disdain for and prejudice against many of the non-Muslim places and peoples he visits, he does display a great deal of respect for the city of Athens ("the abode of sages") and for ancient Greek philosophers and physicians, such as Pythagoras, Hippocrates, Socrates, Plato, Aristotle, Galen, and Ptolemy. Evliya describes Athens as a dynamic place, well populated and prosperous with a wide range of fine arts and crafts. He states that those who visit the city are amazed by its many white marble monuments—wonders that can be found nowhere else on Earth.[51]

Post-classical literary references to the Tower appear in accounts beginning in the fifteenth century. Most are exceedingly brief and vary as to whether an author focuses on the classical or Christian phase of the monument. Evliya reflects all of the Tower's cultural connections in his terminology when, labeling the Octagon "Plato's Pavilion", he describes its classical architecture and sculpture, makes note of the Christian burial, and says that it was a meeting place near the mosque for "learned men". Since Evliya was a devout Muslim and Greeks in Athens generally attained a very low level of education in the Ottoman period, he would likely be using the term "learned men" specifically

48. Evliya's career in data collection began in 1635 when, at 21 years of age, he was hired by Sultan Mehmed IV (ruled 1648–1687) to survey Istanbul's buildings. Evliya's count identified 74 imperial mosques, 1,985 vizir's mosques, 6,990 mosques of town's quarters, 6,000 dervish cells, 557 *tekkes*, and 6,665 prayer spaces; see Lifchez (1992) 89.

49. Dankoff and Kim (2010) passim, esp. 51–52.

50. *Seyahatname*, vol. 8, 250b-257a. Two of his sources are believed to be *The History of Yanvan*, an unknown Arabic work he cites that probably dates to the tenth century, and the eleventh century Persian epic poem by Firdawsi, *The Book of Kings* (*Shahnama*). See Pallis (1951) 62; Dankoff, et al. (2004) 27; Dankoff and Kim (2010) xxi, 278–291.

51. Evliya's respect for ancient Athens mirrors the opinion of the great sultan, Mehmed II (ruled 1451–1481), who spent four days in the city in August 1458 after his conquest of Greece. According to his official historian (Kritoboulos III.51 and 52), Mehmed was called a "Philhellene", a man who was amazed by the "city of philosophers", the classical monuments, and its ancient and contemporary citizens.

for Islamic, not Christian, scholars. Whether by "meeting place" he is saying that they gathered inside the building or in the open area in front of the Tower is not clear.

Evliya's statement about the burial is limited, but it contains information that should be evaluated regarding whether it has some merit as to reliability. It should be noted that the content of his travel book demonstrates that he attempts to inspect the interior as well as the exterior of buildings he visits. His observations show him to be detail-oriented and exceedingly interested in monuments' architecture, paintings, sculpture, and other furnishings. Two of his observations on the Tower are strong indications that he was able to go inside the building and that he did so.

First, Evliya describes in depth images on the ceiling:

> The twelve segments of the dome are laid out according to the twelve constellations of the zodiac. In one segment is depicted the constellation of Ares, the mansion of Mars, retrograde, fiery. In another is Taurus, the mansion of Venus, earthy. In another is Gemini, the mansion of Mercury, airy. In another is Cancer, the mansion of the Moon, watery. In another is Sagittarius, the mansion of Jupiter, fiery. In another is Capricorn, the mansion of Saturn, earthy. In another is Aquarius, the mansion of Saturn, airy. In the twelfth segment is Pisces, the mansion of Jupiter, watery. Thus the seven planets relating to these constellations and the influences of the other stars are depicted. It is a unitary, instructional pavilion of well-wrought marble in twelve segments, at the level of manifest magic."[52]

Evidence regarding the geometric structure of the ceiling and extant paint on its surface lend support to the accuracy of Evliya's account. And as far as can be determined, he is the only visitor in the Ottoman period who can be documented as having examined the interior of the Octagon. Another comment, very brief, from the following decade describes the structure as beautiful on the outside but filthy as a sewer inside.[53] It is possible, however, that this author may have done little more than peek inside, with or without the aid of a torch, although the statement does suggest the building was not well cared for when he saw it. It is not necessarily surprising Evliya did not mention any conditions that were less than pleasant, if indeed the Tower was in need of cleaning. He had traveled so widely to so many primitive places that he would have been accustomed to a certain amount of debris in and around monuments he explored. He was in awe of the ancient buildings in Athens, and that was his primary emotional reaction to them.

Second, this Turkish traveler identifies the saint honored at the site simply as Philip the Greek, information he gleaned from a chronogram in Greek (a language he could read) written on either end of the casket.

The name Philip was borne by several Macedonian kings who ruled between the fourth and second centuries BC and died in northern Greece. The most notable of

52. Dankoff and Kim (2010) 289.
53. Wachsmuth (1874), vol. 1, "Brief des Jesuiten Jacques Paul Babin an den Abbé Pecoil in Lyon," 745–63, esp. 757.

the dynasty was Philip II, the father of Alexander the Great. Along with the fact that Philip II was buried in Macedonia, there is nothing to recommend this pagan monarch as the focus of a Christian cult. Taking into consideration Evliya's beliefs regarding (a) the descent of the Greek people through the royal line of David, (b) the founding of the city of Athens by Solomon, (c) his identification of Philip II of Macedon as a fifth-generation descendant of Solomon, (d) his deep respect for the Greek historical luminaries he mentions including Philip II, (e) his great admiration for the physical remains of ancient Athenian culture, and (f) his general disinterest in the Christian faith and its followers, it is impossible to consider that Evliya might be equating the man buried in the Tower with Philip II. The above points of fact, as well as his treatment of other renowned classical figures in his book, suggest that if he believed the relics were those of the father of Alexander the Great, Evliya would have specifically identified "Philip" as the Macedonian king and would have expressed wonder at being in his presence.

Several saints named Philip who are listed in the Christian calendar have no obvious connection with Athens. Saint Philip of Agira was a missionary to Sicily, where he died in AD 103. Saint Philip of Gortyna was bishop of that Cretan city during the reign of Marcus Aurelius (AD 161–180). Saint Philip of Heracleia was martyred in Thrace in AD 304.

Could the person to whom Evliya refers be an unknown and undocumented Greek saint named Philip? While that is possible, it seems unlikely that the casket in this imposing marble octagon in the center of Byzantine Athens contained relics of a saint so minor that no record of him in church annals has come down to us.

The Apostle Philip and Athens

Is it possible, then, that the relics of this martyr may have belonged not to a Greek-born saint but instead to the Greek-speaking and Greek-named saint Philip the Apostle? One might reasonably assume that if even a small number of an apostle's bones were entombed in Athens, this information would appear somewhere in the historical records. While there is no direct evidence that the martyr was the Apostle Philip, the possibility merits examination.

Along with the chronogram having been written in Greek, Evliya's beliefs regarding the origin of the Greeks and the founding of Athens could have provided a logical basis in his mind for defining as Greek a Palestinian-born man who was buried in Athens. That Evliya provided a meticulously detailed description of the painted ceiling but did not clarify the identity of the person whose relics were interred in the Tower follows his pattern of expressing little interest in or respect for New Testament history and its saints.[54] In a discussion of the Greek language in his book, Evliya includes an incomplete and incorrect list of the names of Jesus' apostles (Simon, Paul, Peter, Andrew, John, Luke, Mark, Jacob, and Thomas); Philip is not among them. Evliya

54. Dankoff and Kim (2010) 288–93.

does, however, refer to Jesus as the Prophet and the Beloved of God. Evliya provides a lengthy and detailed description of the Acropolis and the Parthenon, which at this point had been converted into a mosque, but he offers only the following few words about Christian churches in Athens: "There are a total of 300 houses of idol-worship, and 3,000 priests and monks."

The Apostle Philip, who was from Bethsaida on the northwest shore of the Sea of Galilee, traveled widely, preaching throughout Asia Minor. His mission was to evangelize among the Gentiles, that is, the Greeks. According to Christian tradition and as related in the fourth-century non-canonical *Acts of Philip,* Book 2, he also visited Athens where he preached and founded a church during a two-year stay.[55] Philip later returned to Asia where he was crucified and buried in Phrygian Hierapolis. His grave is believed by the excavator of the site, Francesco D'Andria, to have been located in a small church building near the hill where Philip died.[56] In the early fifth century, a monumental square martyrium was built on the presumed site of Philip's execution, and the saint's relics may have been moved to the vast octagonal chamber at the building's center. In the sixth century, the city suffered from a number of invasions during which the martyrium was destroyed by fire. Hierapolis was demolished by an earthquake in the mid-seventh century.[57]

After the Apostle Philip's martyrium burned, all or at least a large number of his bones were translated from Hierapolis to Constantinople, where they were deposited in the Church of the Holy Apostles and the Church of Saint Artemisius.[58] A significant number of his relics were translated again to Rome, where they were entombed along with those of James the Lesser in the Basilica dei Santi Apostoli, which had been dedicated by Pope John III in 563. A tenth-century document provides evidence that a church dedicated to the apostle had been built in Constantinople, probably in the area of Topkapi near the martyrium of the twin saints Florus and Laurus, and consequently it would have housed some of the apostle's relics.[59] An arm bone of Philip came into

55. The founding of a "church" in the Early Christian period is a reference to the congregation of believers and not the construction of a building.

The *Acts of Philip* comprises fifteen labeled "acts" and the martyrdom of the apostle. Scholars have traditionally considered the document to be of secondary quality and comparatively unimportant to the study of early Christianity; see James (1955) passim, esp. 439–42. In the most recent and thorough re-analysis, however, Matthews draws a quite different conclusion. He also refutes the argument by some scholars that there are two Philips described in the New Testament and other early Christian literature, i.e., Philip the Apostle and Philip the Evangelist; see Matthews (2002) passim, esp. 2–3, 33–34, 65, 95–128, 162–63, 171, 216–17.

56. Limberis (2011) 88–94. On July 27, 2011, the Turkish news agency Anadolu reported that Italian archaeologist Francesco D'Andria, the director of excavations at Hierapolis, announced he had discovered what he believes to be the original tomb of Philip in a newly revealed church. D'Andria states that the design of the tomb and the writings on its walls definitively convince him it belonged to the martyred apostle of Jesus.

57. Verzone (1978) 849–55; D'Andria (2001) 111–13.

58. Preger (1975) 275: *Πάτρια Κωνσταντινουπόλεως* III, 189; Kirsch (1911) 799.

59. Wortley (2009a) 371–73, nn. 55 and 59.

the possession of Maria Komnenos, niece of the Byzantine emperor and wife of the king of Jerusalem, in the twelfth century. It was sent to Florence in 1205, where it still resides in the baptistery.[60]

This pattern of movement of bones believed to have belonged to important biblical figures from one Christian church to another was established early in the Byzantine period after a large number of important relics had been translated from Jerusalem and elsewhere to Constantinople in the fourth and fifth centuries. Included were those attributed to Samuel, Isaiah, Zechariah, Joseph, John the Baptist, Andrew, Luke, Timothy, Lawrence, and Stephen.[61] Saints' relics were commonly acquired through gift giving in order to build bonds between Christian communities, a practice that was first given impetus by Ambrose, the Bishop of Milan, in the late fourth century. This created "a new form of the cult of martyrs which was no longer connected with the place of their martyrdom or their tomb, but with the place where their relics were deposed."[62] The fragmentation of a skeleton was not believed to diminish the value of the bones. In fact, the process of sharing relics greatly increased the prestige of the main cult and strengthened smaller or weaker churches.[63] Brown describes the process: "Translations—the movement of relics to people—and not pilgrimages—the movement of people to relics—hold the center of the stage in late-antique and early-medieval piety. . . ."[64] In such situations, the martyr narrative at the new site often would consist not just of the martyrdom (*passio*) but also of the journey (*translatio*) and the arrival (*adventus*), telling the story of how the relics came to their new home.

At the time when the major assemblage of the Apostle Philip's relics was sent to Rome, is it possible that some of his bones were also sent to Athens and deposited in the Tower? Its octagonal room would certainly call to mind the great octagonal chamber in the martyrium at Hierapolis. Also, the symbol of Philip is the Latin cross. As described above, this form of cross is engraved on the east interior wall of the Tower. This may merely be an indication of the sanctification of this once-pagan monument, but one must take into consideration that here it may specifically identify the saint.

Byzantine Athens

If relics belonging to such a consequential figure as the Apostle Philip were housed within the Tower, is there an explanation for why there is no mention of his cult in extant documents aside from Evliya's commentary? This would seem to be a notable lapse in the documentary record. Examination of the following points will allow evaluation of the question: (a) What was the status of Athens in the centuries following Late

60. Cornelison (2004) 642.
61. Mango (1990) 52–53 and n. 11, 56 and nn. 32 and 33, 60; Limberis (1994) 52, 59.
62. Spieser (2001) Ch. 6, passim, esp. p. 11.
63. Holum and Vikan (1979) 115–20; Geary (1986) 169–83; Geary (1990) 4, 7, 29–34; Grig (2004) 86–87.
64. Brown (1981) 88–89.

Antiquity? (b) How did the overwhelming importance to worshippers of the cult of the Virgin Mary and the Christian Parthenon, when compared to other local churches and religious monuments, influence the historical record? (c) Can much of the blame for the lack of information about the martyrium in the Octagon be related in general to insufficient documentation about churches and relics in the city?

By the seventh century—250 years after the Cappadocian Fathers were in residence—Christian Athens, by comparison with the classical period, was a small city in decline that no longer attracted students and travelers in the numbers it once had. During the eight and a half centuries until the Ottoman Turks took control in 1458, Athens' economy and its reputation as a pilgrimage site waxed and waned as Greece suffered from a number of invasions and military occupations. First-person written accounts of the Late Antique and medieval city are rare, incomplete, and inconsistent.[65] Thus, there is much we do not know about Athens during this period.

Medieval Athens can be divided into three periods: the Dark Ages (seventh–ninth centuries), a period of decline; the middle Byzantine (tenth–twelfth centuries), a period of recovery; and Frankish/Catalan/Florentine rule (thirteenth–fifteenth centuries), a period of decline followed by a nascent recovery.[66]

In the Dark Ages, Athens suffered a severe decline as a result of repeated foreign incursions. The city during this period was no longer known for its renowned visitors and residents, and it is rarely mentioned in contemporary written sources. As the site, however, of one of the most important Christian cults and church buildings in the Byzantine Empire—the Parthenon church dedicated to the Virgin Mary—Athens continued to function as a minor administrative center. Emperor Constans II, his army, and many members of his court spent the winter of 662/3 there. In addition, in the late eighth and early ninth centuries, the city supplied two queens to the Byzantine monarchy in Constantinople, Eirene and her niece Theophano.

In the middle Byzantine period, Athens was part of the military governorship (*theme*) of Hellas, whose capital was Thebes. The betterment of Athens' economic and political status is reflected in the increased size of the city, the number of newly built churches, and the elevation of the local orthodox church from a bishopric to an archbishopric and finally to a metropolitan bishopric. The powerful emperor Basil II, in celebration of his military victory over the Bulgars, made a special trip to Athens in 1018 during which he dedicated the spoils of the war to the Virgin Mary in the cathedral on the Acropolis.[67] The historical accounts for this period are decidedly incomplete, however.

In the few decades before and then during Frankish rule, Athens went into decline again. Michael Choniates, the distinguished scholar and last metropolitan bishop of Byzantine Athens (1182–1204), described the city as a small impoverished town. The

65. Kaldellis (2009) 61.
66. Kazanaki-Lappa (2002) 639–42.
67. Kaldellis (2009) 81–84.

urban center had been reduced again to the area around the Acropolis after Athens suffered an attack in the Fourth Crusade in 1204. Two centuries later (in 1387) when the Acciaiuoli family of Florence had assumed control, evidence shows Athens to be improving economically, although the Italian notary Niccolò da Martoni, on a return trip to Capua from the Holy Lands, describes the city (in 1395) as a small town consisting of approximately one thousand houses.[68]

The Importance of the Christian Parthenon and the Scarcity of Literary References to Other Christian Shrines

While medieval sources are severely lacking in detailed and reliable information, evidence shows Athens to have been a religiously significant Christian city in the Byzantine Empire, a status due entirely to the fact that it was the site of the most important church building in the empire—the Christian Parthenon, the cathedral of Athens (see Appendix 2). It was referred to by local residents and by foreign visitors as the Church of the Mother of God(Theotokos), the Holy Virgin of Athens(Panagia Atheniotissa), or, most commonly, simply "the Church". The Parthenon is rarely mentioned in ancient Greek and Roman sources, but it is frequently discussed in Byzantine literature. In fact, not only is Mary worshipped, but the building itself appears to have been the subject of adoration. Pilgrims who came to Athens did so specifically to visit and pray at the Church of the Theotokos. Christian inscriptions on the architectural members of the Parthenon, dating to the period between the early seventh and the fifteenth centuries, are more numerous than on any other building in the Byzantine Empire.

In his examination of the literature dating from the tenth and eleventh centuries, Kaldellis concludes that because of the prominence of the Atheniotissa, the city was the fourth most important Byzantine pilgrimage site of the period (along with Constantinople, Thessaloniki, and Ephesus), although it was not the primary destination for non-Greek travelers—the wandering saints and pilgrims on their way to Constantinople, the Holy Lands, and other destinations.[69] Again, it was the cult of Mary and the great church itself—and not relics or icons or miracles—that were the focus of non-Greek pilgrims in Athens. Other Christian cults and monuments in the city seem to have been given little consideration.

As an example of the deficiencies in written sources from this period, one need only consider the quality of information regarding relics said to be within the Christian Parthenon. Saints' relics in the Cathedral are mentioned in the literature, but the documentation is inconsistent and confusing. The accounts of the relics of (the possibly legendary) Saint Martinianos, who was from Caesarea in Palestine and was believed

68. Setton (1944) passim; Paton (1951) 5, 32; Setton (1975) ch. 3, 204.

69. Pilgrimage to the Holy Lands by Byzantine Christians became far less common after the sixth century. Constantinople, as the "new Jerusalem", was the primary pilgrimage site due to the large number of relics, churches, and monasteries, as well as its renown as the city of Constantine's conversion; see Kaldellis (2009) passim, esp. 2, 11, 18, 69–71, 75–80, 110, 167.

to have died in Athens in the fifth century, are particularly instructive. One version of the compilation of orthodox saints' lives, the *Synaxarion,* states that Saint Phantinos (tenth century) went to Athens to pray in the Parthenon and to embrace the relics of Saint Martinianos (which, however, are not specifically described as being in the Parthenon). In a second version of the *Synaxarion,* it is the relics of Saint Andreas that Phantinos desires to hold. A third version has Phantinos visiting the Parthenon but does not mention any relics. Niccolò da Martoni, the Italian notary from Capua, describes his visit to the Theotokos (in 1395) and lists relics he saw there, which include those of neither Martinianos nor Andreas.[70]

According to Evliya, at the time of his visit in 1668 there were three hundred churches in Athens.[71] Descriptions of the Christian Parthenon, however, constitute the overwhelming number of references to churches in extant sources. Other Christian monuments in Athens command little attention. Thus, it is not completely surprising that the Christian Tower and its cult would go unmentioned, eclipsed by the adoration of the Theotokos and the extreme focus on her cult and her church.

The fact that the Tower remained so well preserved throughout the centuries is in itself a statement indicative of ongoing use, however. Ancient structures converted for Christian or other contemporary employment survived in greater numbers and in better condition than did abandoned classical buildings, which were subsequently looted for their materials or decayed through disuse and the vagaries of time. In the case of the Late Antique Octagon, the building is attested to have been in service to the local religious community by the crosses on the exterior and interior walls, the Byzantine wall paintings, and the proximal Christian graves. The well-preserved condition of the building demonstrates that it likely did so throughout the Byzantine period.

As for the relics of Philip, one might assume that those belonging to an apostle—albeit one of the lesser of the twelve brethren—would certainly command some attention from locals and foreigners alike. It is possible, however, that they may have been overshadowed by the fact that many important relics related to Christ's life and death, Mary's life and death, as well as relics of Old Testament, New Testament, early Christian, and medieval saints, including some belonging to Philip, had been translated to numerous religious sites across the Christian world, including larger and more dynamic cities in the eastern and western Mediterranean region—cosmopolitan centers such as Constantinople, Thessaloniki, Rome, and Milan.

In the twelfth century, visits of secular travelers to Athens were becoming more numerous than those of Christian pilgrims, the opposite of evidence for the tenth and eleventh centuries. It was at this time that there arose an inchoate interest in the city's classical remains.[72] Even so, the Tower continues to be missing from extant written sources. Archibishop of Athens Michael Choniates, who lived on the Acropolis,

70. Paton (1951) 31; Kaldellis (2009) 143 and n. 65, 171.
71. Dankoff and Kim (2010) 288.
72. Kaldellis (2009) 129, 191–92.

expresses great love for the renowned Athens of the classical world yet references few ancient buildings. He does inform us that the Lysicrates Monument was called the "Lantern of Demosthenes", and that the Heliaia, the Peripatos encircling the slopes of the Acropolis, and the Lyceum were no longer extant. He does not, however, mention the Octagon or most other monuments from antiquity.[73]

This lacuna in the historical record does not come to an end until the fifteenth century when, in the few decades before the Turkish conquest and then during Ottoman rule, the monument makes brief appearances in a number of first-person accounts produced by secular and religious visitors to Athens. In these, appellations of the Tower vacillate between its classical and Christian identities. Thus, to a number of European Humanists, the Octagon of the classical period was of particular interest, although it was frequently identified by erroneous nomenclature. Others who viewed the building as part of Byzantine Athens labeled the structure a church.

The Christian Tower in Ottoman Period

Athens fell under Ottoman control in 1458, and the city's population over time became a mixture of Orthodox Greeks and Turkish and Albanian Muslims.[74] The Acropolis served as a military fortress and the residence of the Turkish governor. The Christian Parthenon was transformed into a mosque. The area around the Tower continued as the commercial and administrative center of the city, only with the addition of mosques, madrassas, and other Ottoman and Islamic institutions. For example, in the northeast corner of the Roman Agora, still the main market area, stood the Fetiye mosque, built at the time of the Ottoman conquest. The Octagon appears to have been well integrated into this multicultural environment, for as mentioned above, Evliya notes that it housed a Christian cult and was also a meeting place for learned men (i.e., Muslim scholars).

It has generally been thought that the Tower must have been vacant for some considerable time between its Christian and Muslim phases, during which it gradually became filled with debris.[75] The evidence does not support this opinion, however. Several fifteenth-century visitors describe the structure as a church, an indication that it was not abandoned when they saw it. In 1668 Evliya was able to enter the building and view the martyr's casket, which, he is told, Christians visit on the saint's feast day. This report that the casket was in situ signifies that the floor was not covered by meters of debris, and the visits on the martyr's feast day are an indication that the cult was still active. I suspect that the building would have been untenanted only for a relatively short period at the end of the seventeenth century and in the first several decades of the eighteenth century at a time when almost all life in Athens came to a halt.

73. Setton (1975) 204.
74. By the mid-seventeenth century, Athens is estimated to have had approximately 2,000 houses (600 belonging to Turks), with a resident population of ca. 8,000–10,000 people; see Paton (1951) 11.
75. Von Freeden (1983) 18–24; Kienast (2014) 152.

In 1687, a little more than two hundred years after the Ottoman Turks seized Athens, an alliance of European nations sent a combined military force under the command of the Venetian Francesco Morosini to recapture Greece for the Christian West.[76] Once the Peloponnese came under his control, he sailed from Corinth to Piraeus and marched on Athens. On September 26 during an assault on the Acropolis, gunpowder stored by the Turks in the Parthenon exploded, severely damaging the venerable temple. The Turks surrendered the city three days later, and their soldiers and civilians were deported to Smyrna.

Morosini's army was too small and the funds too meager for an ongoing defense of Athens by the Europeans, however. Also, a devastating plague broke out in Attica and the Peloponnese. Morosini attempted to control the spread of disease in the city by burning the houses of those who had died. In spite of his attempts, contagion remained rampant. Consequently, he decided to move the army and the population of Athens to what he believed would be a more healthful environment on nearby islands and in the area around Corinth. By April 8, 1688, Athens was almost entirely empty. The Venetian alliance had held the city for 197 days. The siege had accomplished nothing but inflicting more damage than all other assaults combined—by Sulla, the Heruli, the Avars, and others—over the previous eighteen centuries.

Athens remained essentially deserted for almost three years. In 1691, with the European forces' hold on areas of southern Greece either weak or abandoned,[77] Sultan Ahmed II offered amnesty to Greek civilians who were willing to move back to the city. They were promised restoration of their property and cessation of taxation for three years. The majority of Athenians returned home. The city was in ruins, a very different place from what it had been only thirteen years earlier. Hundreds of houses had been burned. Broken blocks of marble and limestone from damaged and destroyed monuments cluttered the streets. The ground was deep with debris.

I think it likely that most of the damage to the Tower documented by Stuart and Revett occurred during the Venetian siege and its aftermath. As stated above, they found the two northwest porch columns broken but in situ. Fragments of the entablature and a column from the northeast porch were on the ground nearby. A number of architectural elements were missing including, the northeast entablature, one of the porch columns, the capitals from both porches, the upper courses of the semicircular annex, parts of the balustrade (segments of which were found outside the Tower and in the Roman Agora), and the three freestanding columns from the main chamber.

76. Wachsmuth (1874) 14–20; Setton (1991) 304–43, 347, 365.

77. The Venetian military alliance held on in the Peloponnese (the Morea) until Ottoman reconquest in 1716. Turkish residents (who had fled to Chios, the Anatolian mainland, and elsewhere) were, like the Athenians, provided incentives to move back to their former homes in Greece. Three decades of Ottoman-Venetian conflict in the late seventeenth century exacerbated a population decline across southern Greece that had been on-going for a century, and which did not begin to reverse until the eighteenth century. See Zarinebaf (2005) passim, esp. 15 and n. 31, 18; Zarinebaf, Davis, and Bennet (2005) 212.

Some of these items may have been purposefully carried off for reuse elsewhere in rebuilding the city. The fact that sections of the balustrade were removed from the edifice means that they were accessible and not buried beneath meters of debris. Thus, it is most likely at the time of the city's reconstruction when much of the debris and rubble was deposited in and filled the lower portion of the now partially buried building.

Over the next several decades Athens was gradually made habitable. Open areas between the houses and the town walls were extensive enough that they were planted with grain. A mosque was rebuilt inside the heavily damaged Parthenon but was much smaller than its predecessor (Ill. 43). The lower town, north of the Acropolis, still the commercial and administrative center of the Ottoman city although much more limited in size, was enlivened by several bazaars. A madrassa was built across from the entrances to the Octagon.

Thus, the only period during which the Christian Tower seems to have ceased to function as a religious monument up to this time is in the decades following 1688. At some point in the second quarter of the eighteenth century, the Mevlevi order of whirling dervishes[78] took possession of the Octagon and converted it into a Muslim lodge (*tekke*), a practice they had carried out with Christian buildings elsewhere.[79]

Literary References to the Tower

Among the earliest and most important documents that mentions the Tower subsequent to Varro and Vitruvius was produced at the end of the medieval period by the Italian merchant and antiquarian Cyriacus of Ancona, who first visited Athens in April 1436; a second visit followed in 1444. Cyriacus filled his notebooks with observations of the city, drew a number of classical monuments and pieces of sculpture, and copied fifty-two ancient inscriptions, several of which are the only extant examples. The Tower, labeled by him the "Temple of the Winds," is described merely as a marble octagon with images of eight gods, whose names he transcribes. In one manuscript copy in the section that precedes his passage about the Tower, Cyriacus lists twelve winds and gives their names in both Greek and Latin.[80] One wonders if he may have had in mind the monument in Rome described by Cetius, which perhaps he saw (if it was still extant) during his visits to that city in the previous two decades.

Another mid-fifteenth-century commentary by the Anonymous of the Ambrosian Library, which contains a brief description of the Tower and its relief sculpture, is the earliest extant written account that labels the building a Greek church.[81] The

78. The sect was founded by the thirteenth century mystic Mevlana Celaleddin Rumi.

79. For example, in the fifteenth century, a large number of Christian churches and monasteries in Istanbul were given by the sultans to dervish orders for conversion into *tekkes*. See Lifchez (1992) 80; Kreiser (1992) 51.

80. Bodnar (1960) 35–38, 83 n. 5; 84 and n. 2, 98–99 and n. 1; Bodnar (1970) 96–105.

81. Ziebarth (1899) 77; Bodnar (1970a) 96–105, Bodnar (1970b) 188–199.

same designation for the Octagon is found in a document based on notes that were composed on July 12, 1466, eight years after the Ottoman conquest of Athens. On that day the Venetian Navy, under the command of Vettore Cappello, attempted to recapture the city. Cappello found the Acropolis impregnable and gave up the siege within a day. Before sailing away, however, one of his (anonymous) Venetian compatriots made a tour of the lower city and its monuments including the Tower, which he describes as a church.[82] From the same time period, a third reference to the Tower as a Greek church was offered by the Milan Anonymous, the author most likely being Condottiere Bertolo da Ca' d'Este, writing in about 1470.[83]

From this time forward references to the Tower for the most part either mention the marble octagon and its relief sculpture with no appellation or connect the building to a famous person from ancient Athens, reflecting in their erroneous nomenclature the Humanist interest in classical antiquity and its monuments. As Paton points out, the fabricated classical appellations applied to various ancient monuments beginning in the fifteenth century are probably not the survival of a popular tradition; rather, associating monuments with famous historical figures was merely a means by which local Athenians impressed foreign visitors. For example, two documents from the second half of the fifteenth century by authors whose names we do not know—the Vienna Anonymous and the Paris Anonymous—refer to the Octagon as the School of Socrates and the shrine or grave of Socrates.[84] According to François Arnaud, a ship captain who sailed from Marseilles to Athens in 1602, the monument was known as the House of Pythagoras.[85] Later in the century the German traveler Johann Georg Transfeldt, who lived in the city in 1674 and 1675, mentions the Tower without naming it, merely stating its location in the center of "modern" Athens (i.e., north of the Acropolis).[86] Also in the 1670s in accounts compiled by Capuchins,[87] in which one might expect them to mention the Christian history of the building, the monks merely reflect the common contemporary classification of the Tower as a classical monument and identify the building as the Tomb of Socrates or the Prison of Socrates. They describe it as originally having been built by ancient Athenians as a symbol of regret over their treatment of the philosopher, with the winds representing the capriciousness of those who had sought his death. In 1699the French ambassador to Constantinople Charles, Comte de Ferriol, who visited Athens on his way to the Ottoman court, similarly describes the

82. Miller (1908) 468 and n. 2.
83. Ziebarth (1899) 82.
84. Wachsmuth (1874) 731–44, esp. 731 and n. 2, 743 and n. 2; Paton (1951) 15, 176.
85. Paton (1951) 52 and n. 13.
86. Wachsmuth (1874) 70–71 and n. 2; Setton (1975) ch. 5, 281.
87. The Capuchins founded a mission in Athens in 1658, which remained active until the Greek War of Independence. In 1669 they purchased a group of buildings for their headquarters into which the Lysicrates Monument had been incorporated. They identified the ancient tholos as "the Lantern of Demosthenes", and believed it to have been originally a secret chamber that was once part of the orator's house, which he used as a study. See Paton (1951) 10 and n. 11, 13–15 and n. 21.

edifice as the Tomb of Socrates or the Tower of Socrates, but he labels the relief figures as representations of the abundance of life's necessities.[88]

In the book *Athènes ancienne et moderne* (Paris, 1675), the Tower for the first time since the classical period is referred to as the Horologion of Andronikos and identified as the monument discussed by Vitruvius. Its author, Guillet de Saint-George, had never seen the building in person, however. His physical description of the Octagon is based on notes compiled by Capuchin monks. For his perceptive conclusion regarding the monument's identification in antiquity, he relied on an analysis of the works of classical authors by the contemporary Dutch scholar Johannes Meursius.[89]

A more modern methodological approach to examination of the Tower was presented a few years later in *A Journey into Greece* (London, 1678) by the Frenchman Jacob Spon and the Englishman George Wheler, both of whom spent a month and a half in Athens in 1676, less than a decade after Evliya's visit. Their entry on the Horologion, which they call the Temple of the Eight Winds, includes a general description of the architecture with detailed drawings of the reliefs. Spon, who had broad knowledge of the ancient sources (and possibly of the book by de Saint-George), mentions Vitruvius' discussion of the monument, including that the builder was Andronikos Kyrrhestes.[90]

A century later in 1751, when Stuart and Revett excavated the Tower, the presence of human bones in the fill led them to conclude that the building had served in the post-classical period as a Christian church.[91] In the early nineteenth century Edward Clarke, a renowned and widely traveled English scientist who was familiar with Stuart and Revett's publication, took a much more expansive position than other chroniclers—a position with which I concur. Clarke thinks that the Tower may have been a religious monument throughout its entire history. He states that Christians once used the building as a church and posits that it was also probably "one of the sacred structures of the ancient city and, as a place of worship, served for other purposes than that of merely indicating the direction of the Winds, the Seasons, and the Hours."[92]

88. Paton (1951) 169 and n. 37.
89. Paton (1951) 10 n. 11.
90. Wheler and Spon (1682) 395–97.
91. Stuart and Revett (1762) 18; Stuart and Revett (1825) 43.
92. Clarke (1818) 269.

III

THE MUSLIM TOWER

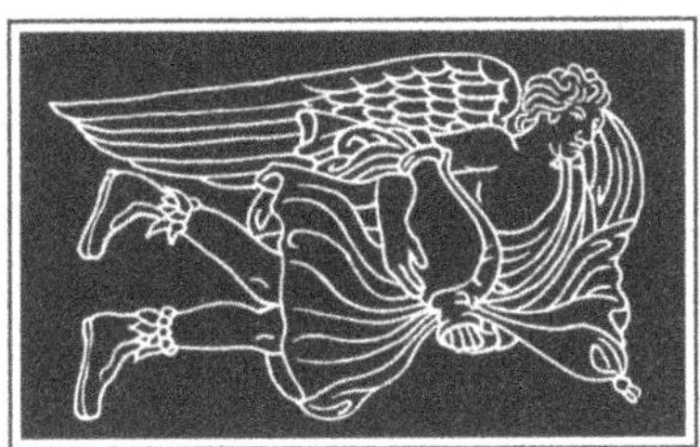

Whirling Dervishes and the Tower

In the process of creating a fortress for their armed garrison and a residence for the military governor, the Ottoman Turks found it expedient and practicable to convert the large well-built structures on the Acropolis to suit their diverse needs. They appear to have readapted few classical buildings elsewhere in the city, however. Their preference for constructing new mosques, madrassas, hammams, imarets, and other Ottoman buildings may have been particularly influenced by their architectural requirements, which often included domed chambers and series of rooms grouped around open courtyards.[1]

The Tower was one of the relatively few classical buildings located in the city proper converted to Muslim use. The Sufi sect of whirling dervishes transformed it into a Muslim lodge (*tekke*) between 1735 and 1749. Evidence for such precise dating is contained in two illustrations, the first by Richard Pococke and the second by Richard Dalton (Ills. 38, 39). Pococke's drawing of the interior of the Octagon, made in 1735, shows a rough and uneven pile of soil rising to the first cornice. Dalton's sketch of the interior, made fourteen years later, portrays the surface at the level of the first cornice as smooth, thus indicating that the wood floor on which the dervishes danced had been installed by that time.[2] It was removed two years later during the excavation of the monument by Stuart and Revett.

James Stuart's illustration of the area in which the Tower stood, published in 1762 (Ill. 40), depicts Mevlevi dervishes (to the left of the monument's door) and Christian

1. Two examples of such new construction existed in the neighborhood of the Horologion. The Fethiye Djami (Mosque of the Conquest) was built in 1456 in the open area of the Roman Agora, and covers most of the ruins of a seventh century Christian basilica (see Appendix 2). The mosque is entered through a deep porch comprised of an arcaded façade with five domed bays. The interior is a single square room surmounted in the center by a large shallow dome. At each of the four corners are smaller domes, with half-domes in between, supported by four large columns. A madrasa, established in 1721 to the north of the Octagon, was entered through a large domed lecture hall that also served as the school's mosque. Beyond was a courtyard with colonnades on the east and south sides, behind which were small rooms that served as the students' living quarters.
2. Pococke (1745) pl. 76; Dalton (1791) fig. 53.

women (in front of the wall to the right) seemingly going about their business in mutual forbearance, even though they are not only of different religions and cultures, but are also members of dominant and subject populations. Stuart's sketch also shows the building to be embedded in a very crowded neighborhood. As the local headquarters of the Mevlevi Sufis, the Octagon would have made some contribution to daily activities in this busy area of Ottoman Athens.

When the two Dilettanti first saw the Tower in 1751, the surrounding ground level was at a height that buried the building up to the middle of the door frames. Its roof was crowned by a wood finial in the shape of a turban. The interior was filled with 2.10 meters of rubble, which the dervishes had covered with a deal platform in order to provide a surface on which to carry out their whirling dance. This must not have been a very satisfactory situation, however, for when the Englishmen asked the head of the order, Sheikh Mustafa, for permission to remove the flooring and clear the debris in order to carry out a study of the Tower, permission was readily granted.[3] Twenty-seven hundred cubic feet (76.46 cubic meters) of soil and stone were removed, exposing the building to its exterior foundations and interior marble pavement. This constituted ca. 4.50–5.00 meters of earth being excavated from the exterior on every side except the northeast; there Stuart and Revett needed to excavate only ca. 3.00–3.75 meters of soil, for the upper half of the northeast door had been kept unblocked to allow access to the building. A wall of the house immediately to the rear of the Tower entirely covered the figure of Lips and half of Notos. The Dilettanti were able to convince the owner to tear down and rebuild the wall (with a viewing window) at a further remove in order to expose the reliefs completely. At that point, the architecture and sculpture were documented—measured, described in detail, and illustrated. Then the Octagon was given over once again to the Mevlevis. Ownership of the building remained in their hands until the outbreak of the Greek War of Independence in 1821.

An important moment in the excavations by the Dilettanti—for the purposes of this discussion—was the discovery, as mentioned above, of human bones in the rubble and debris below the level of the first cornice. Stuart and Revett's analysis of this find was expressed as follows: "As the Greeks bury in their churches, the human bones found here seem to indicate that this has once been a Christian church."[4] They provide no further clarification.

This leaves us with the question of whether these were the relics of the Christian martyr or the remains of some hapless Athenian or Turk who had died in the Venetian assault or from the plague. Considering the amount of detail they offer elsewhere in their commentary, the excavators' brief comments here lead to the supposition that they did not recover a complete skeleton, for if they had they probably would have stated so. Thus, this was unlikely to have been a victim of the previous century's

3. Stuart and Revett (1762) 14, 17; Stuart and Revett (1825) 37 and n. *b*, 38, 41. Sheik Mustafa is depicted in Stuart's illustration as the Turkish man with long hair standing to the left of the Tower's entrance.

4. Stuart and Revett (1762) 18; Stuart and Revett (1825) 43.

upheavals. It is not unreasonable to consider whether they may have been the martyr's relics. Stuart and Revett do not report finding the bones in a casket or reliquary, but this does not mean that they had not been in a container originally. While many caskets and reliquaries were of marble or other types of stone, they could also be made from wood. In the mid-sixth century when the relics attributed to the New Testament saints Andrew, Timothy, and Luke were returned to the recently rebuilt Church of the Holy Apostles in Constantinople, their relics were carried in three wood coffins (each inscribed with the saint's name) on the lap of the aged patriarch Menas as he rode through the streets in the imperial carriage. This would have been possible only if these had been relatively small wood boxes of the type seen in the Trier Ivory, containing a few bones each.[5] The martyr's relics in the Tower similarly could have been encased in wood and, after more than half a century of being buried in debris, the box decayed, leaving no trace.

The Tower as a Dervish *Tekke* and Cult Site for a Christian Martyr

The reason why the dervishes converted the Octagon into a *tekke* may have been based merely on the fact that it was in a good location in the center of Ottoman Athens, surrounded by Turkish civic and religious buildings. It is unlikely, however, that they did not know the monument had served a Christian function. Its recent history as a Christian cult site should have been common knowledge, and the placement by the dervishes of a turban finial on its roof is an indication the Mevlevis were cognizant of that history. Among Turkish Muslims a turban is the mark of a burial, and from the early Ottoman period it was their custom to identify the graves of men in this manner.[6]

5. Wortley (2009c) 214–17, 219.

6. The oldest gravestone adorned with a turban in Istanbul dates to 1513; see Laqueur (1992) 284–94, esp. 291.

On illustrated maps of the seventeenth and eighteenth centuries, the Octagon's roof is depicted in a variety of ways, underscoring inconsistencies in minor elements in these early maps. An image of the building, published in 1759, although printed in reverse with the winds flying toward the left, shows no turban or other finial at that time atop the Tower; see Sayer (1759) pl. 10. On other illustrated maps of Athens of the period, where the Octagon's roof can be seen, either no finial is depicted or there is what appears to be a vertical rod; see Omont (1898) 7, pl. 42, #15; 12, pl. 36 (lower); 16, pl. 40, #34. It is possible a vertical rod may have been in place in 1668, for Evliya describes a stylus on the top of the Octagon's roof; see Coronelli's map of 1687 in Omont (1898) 14, pl. 41, #5; Dankoff and Kim (2010) 289. In the slim volume authored by the French Jesuit cleric, Jacques Paul Babin, *Relation de l'état présent de la ville d'Athènes, ancienne capitale de Grèce, bâtie depuis 3400. ans : avec un abregé de son histoire et de ses antiquités* (published by Jacob Spon in Paris in 1675), Plate 1 is a view of the city in which the Tower is visible. On the roof as a finial is an Ottoman crescent. Babin had supplied his artist with a generally realistic representation of Athens that was, however, merely a rough sketch without such minor features; see Paton (1951) 10 n. 11; Omont (1898) 13, pl. 38 (upper left corner). Consequently, this and other small details cannot be considered to be reliable.

It was very important in the dervishes' mystical tradition to carry out their rituals in the spiritual presence of saints, and while *tekkes* took a variety of architectural forms, a saint's tomb was a common component.[7] There is no published account of the dervish Tower being dedicated to a Muslim saint. Thus, it is plausible that the saint they venerated was the Christian martyr identified by Evliya as Philip. For the Mevlevis, knowledge that the Octagon had served as a martyrium would have been a positive feature, and honoring a Christian saint would not have been inappropriate. As a manifestation of their reverence for holy persons from other religious faiths as well as for Muslim saints, the dervishes incorporated traditions from pre-Islamic religious practices into their comprehensive cult. *Tekkes* were frequently built on sites that had a long history of Christian use prior to the Ottoman conquest because the dervishes considered such ground to be holy and the saints' powers to be miraculous.[8]

One can also find Christian architectural components and furnishings incorporated into shrines built for Muslim saints. On the Acropolis of Nacolia in west-central Anatolia, a Byzantine bishopric in the medieval period, stood a monastic church dedicated to the archangel Michael. It was replaced in the thirteenth century by a martyrium for Seyyid Gazi, a Sufi saint of the Bektashi dervish order. Evidence suggests, however, that some part of the church may have remained extant, although possibly in ruins, until the remodeling of the Sufi tomb in the sixteenth century, and that local Christians continued to honor their saint side by side with Muslim worshippers. In the renovated Sufi martyrium a number of Christian elements and motifs were displayed in prominent positions: three mid-fifth-century baptismal fonts were built into the complex, including one in an arched niche in the entrance corridor; a brass vessel (now in the Museum of Turkish and Islamic Art in Istanbul) was adorned with figures depicting both Christian and Islamic themes; and the sarcophagus of the Sufi saint was safeguarded by six candle stands adorned with images of the Virgin Mary.[9]

Even with the Tower's function as a martyrium known, however, it is doubtful that the Mevlevis knew that human remains were in the building when they granted permission for the Dilettanti to excavate. If they had believed relics to be in situ, as Muslims—especially Sufi Muslims—they would not have intentionally permitted the destruction of a tomb, Christian or Muslim.[10] The tone and content of Stuart and Revett's statement about the bones suggests that they, too, did not know prior to excavation

7. Tanman (1992) 131, 165.
8. Lapidus (1992) 28; Goodwin (1992) 62; Tanman (1992) 133.
9. Reuse of spolia from earlier monuments was common in the architecture of this area of Anatolia from Late Antiquity through the early Ottoman period. It was a rare feature, however, in the sixteenth century; see Yürekli (2012) 79 and n. 2; 80 and nn. 11 and 12; 96 and n. 51; 139–40, fig. 3.13. The images of Mary in this Muslim religious building bring to mind the preservation of the apse mosaic depicting the Virgin when the Parthenon was converted from a church into a mosque; see Appendix 2.
10. A further example of the consideration shown by Ottoman Muslims toward the faith of the local Christian community can be found in accounts of the visit of Mehmed II ("the Conqueror") in 1458, after Greece fell to the Turks. As part of his demonstration of respect for ancient and contemporary Athens, the sultan granted full recognition to Orthodox Christianity, its churches and shrines. The sole exceptions were

there was a burial within the Tower. Consequently, in the aftermath of the Ottoman-Venetian war and the abandonment of the city over a number of years, the Octagon may have been in such a state of disrepair, surrounded by and filled with the detritus of the devastating events of the late seventeenth century, that returning residents considered the relics of the martyr to have been lost.

Regarding the building in the context of Sufi architecture, as easily as the Hellenistic Tower was converted to Christian use, it would seem that so, too, it was converted easily for use by the Sufi Muslims. The octagonal shape of the monument—a common element in Christian churches, baptisteries, and martyria—was also a familiar component in *tekke* architecture.[11] And the conical dome recalled the ceiling in the tomb of their founder, Rumi, in Konya.[12] When the Mevlevis chose the structure for renovation as a *tekke,* the composition of the building—its orientation, octagonal shape, and reliefs of the winds—may also have brought to mind the Kaaba in Mecca. In his consideration of certain medieval Arabic texts, King concludes the Kaaba may have been planned in accordance with a wind theory. He notes that these early texts view the world as divided into eight sectors with the Kaaba at the center, and they relate solar and stellar alignments to the directions from which the winds blow. Thus, in comparing the two monuments, King finds that the Tower of the Winds evokes various mathematical and scientific features of the Kaaba, the most holy of Muslim shrines.[13]

The size of the Tower, moreover, would have been a desirable characteristic. *Tekke* mausolea were often larger than other Turkish tombs because building funerary monuments was a stronger tradition within the mystical orders than it was in other parts of Ottoman culture. Among the dervishes, two-storey *tekkes* were common, with a tomb located on the lower level and the meeting hall with a mihrab and a place for prayer on the upper level.

What became of the Tower subsequent to the investigation by Stuart and Revett is documented in a number of first-person accounts by European visitors, most notably the Irish traveler Edward Dodwell, whose text and paintings dating to the early years of the nineteenth century provide valuable details.[14] Illustration 41 depicts the northeast door of the Octagon with numerous pairs of shoes left outside the threshold, as is required before entering a Muslim religious building. The Mevlevis have painted the northeast lintel red and inscribed on it the first pillar of Islam: "There is no God but God and Muhammad is his prophet." On the roof they placed a plaster turban

the churches in the Acropolis fortress, which were closed (access to the mount was barred to all except Muslims); see Babinger (1978) 160–61, 178.

11. For example, the Galata lodge in Istanbul (founded ca. 1451–1481) was a tall, two-storey, octagonal building with graves of Muslim worshippers near its walls; see Lifchez (1992) 107–08; Friedlander (1992) 88.
12. Goodwin (1992) 65.
13. King (1982) 305–06, figs. 1 and 3. The entrance is adjacent to the east corner of the monument. The three pillars inside the structure lie on a northwest-southeast axis.
14. Dodwell (1819) v. 1, 373–77. For other eye-witness accounts, see Chandler (1776) 108–09; Clarke (1818) 268–69; Carey (2003) 166–68.

as a finial.[15] Within the building, a new wood platform was installed atop the lowest interior cornice, supported, one assumes, by newly introduced fill (Ill. 42). Dodwell's text describes the interior walls as having been whitewashed; on them were displayed wood tablets carrying passages from the Quran. A small wood balcony was built on the west wall at the level of the second cornice. Twelve small lamps hung suspended from a chain attached to the keystone in the dome. On the southeast wall was a mihrab (2.25 meters high and 0.40 meters wide) painted with vertical green and red stripes. Within the niche was a Quran, a candle at either side; two green flags of Muhammad stood in front. As described above, a window high in the Octagon's west wall created by the removal of a single ashlar block allowed light to fall in the area of the mihrab. Within the Tower each Friday evening the Mevlevis performed their Sufi rituals, including the whirling dance (the *sema*), accompanied by flutes and drums, while dressed in their religiously symbolic costume—the tall felt hat signifying a tombstone; the black robe, which they flung aside, the grave; and the long, full white skirt, a shroud of resurrection.[16]

It can probably be assumed the Mevlevis had knowledge that the monument once housed a Christian saint's burial, but it can only be surmised whether laying a floor atop the fill was in part intended to create not only a platform for dancing but also an upper and lower storey, with what they believed was an empty tomb beneath their feet. For Sufis, praying to a saint was often facilitated through means of a "salutation window", a hole in the wall that provided contact between worshipper and saint while also prohibiting physical access to the tomb.[17] This raises the question as to whether a missing wall block above the first cornice on the south side of the Octagon's main chamber, creating an opening into the annex, might be a salutation window that provided contact with the saint's now-inaccessible burial site (Ills. 10b, 15).[18] Also to be considered is whether the block removed from the north wall was intended to allow light to fall specifically on this part of the wall. Though the Mevlevis would have preferred to have possessed the relics, even without them they would have believed the saint's spirit still to be in residence.

As for the bones, their fate remains unexplained. Even though Stuart and Revett considered them to be relics of a Christian burial, they do not say whether they returned them to the dervishes or to local Christians for reinterment. Considering the type of information included in their footnotes, one would expect them to mention it if they had done so.

15. The plaster turban, which replaced the earlier wood turban, was removed in 1919 by Orlandos, who returned the Hellenistic acanthus finial to the Tower's roof; see Orlandos (1919) 14–15, fig. 1.
16. For an overview of Mevlevi religious dress and rituals, see Atasoy (1992) 253–68.
17. Lifchez (1992) 75; Tanman (1992) 138–39, 147–49.
18. For additional views of the opening into the annex, see Kienast (2014) fig. 127, pl. 36b.

The Christian Cult and the Basilica of Saint Philip

With the dervishes taking ownership of the Octagon, the cult of Philip as observed by Christians ceased to exist in the building. But if the Tower's saint was Philip the Apostle, this did not mean that he had no Christian cult site in Athens. A church dedicated to him stands near the spot where Book II in the *Acts of Philip* says he preached—in the area north of the Greek Agora.

The date of the original three-aisled basilica is in dispute. Soteriou states without supporting evidence that the original church was built in the ninth century.[19] Bouras, using nineteenth-century drawings and focusing on details of the roofing system, thinks that the original church should be dated to the early thirteenth century.[20] Frantz includes Saint Philip's in a group of three-aisled basilicas she dates between the late fifteenth and late seventeenth centuries, postulating that this church is most likely a sixteenth-century construction.[21]

The earliest illustrations of the building are drawings by Couchaud from 1842 that show the extant building to be in an extremely deteriorated condition due to damage suffered during the Greek War of Independence (1821–1832). By 1866, when Mommsen saw it, the church had been rebuilt.[22] That nineteenth-century structure was dismantled in 1960 and replaced by a new church in 1963, which is the building that stands today. No remains earlier than the basilica that Couchaud sketched were identified in the excavations for the new foundations of the 1963 church.

Cartographical evidence suggests a date for construction of the Basilica of Saint Philip to be some point in the eighteenth century. The fact that the church does not appear on the best maps of the second half of the seventeenth century suggests that the basilica did not exist at the time they were drawn. A map of Athens created by the Capuchin monks ca. 1670 depicts a number of Christian buildings along with classical monuments (including the Tower of the Winds, no. 34).[23] Among them are named churches, monasteries, and hospices. The monks also drew a number of unnamed religious buildings, which are identified merely as "Greek churches" (all labeled no. 15). No church is depicted at the site where the Basilica of Saint Philip stands. Spon's map from 1678 offers a longer list of named churches spread out across Athens and the surrounding countryside.[24] Again, the site of the basilica is empty. A map very similar to the Capuchin map, drawn by Coronelli in 1687, portrays classical monuments (e.g., "Torre di Andronico Cireste o Torre delli Venti", no. 5) and a significant number of

19. Soteriou (1927) 63–65, figs. 49 and 50; Couchaud (1842) pl. 2.
20. Bouras (2010) 240–42, figs. 232–237.
21. Travlos and Frantz (1965) 174–79; Frantz, et al. (1988) 73–74 & n. 119.
22. Couchaud (1842) pl. 2; Mommsen (1868) 105–06, #125.
23. Their original map has not survived, but an exact replica made by La Guilletière five years later, in 1675, is extant. See Omont (1898) 13–16, esp. 14–15; pl. 40.
24. Omont (1898) pl. 42.

churches.[25] The basilica of Saint Philip is not one of them. Thus, this would seem to be an indication that the original building did not exist before the eighteenth century, but was constructed during the period after the Athenians, who had been displaced by Morosini, had returned home to rebuild their city.[26]

---

25. Omont (1898) pl. 41.

26. The altar of the nineteenth century church that was demolished in 1960 contained no bones of the saint. The current basilica does possess a small relic of the apostle, but it is a recent acquisition, a gift from the Augustinian monks of the Abbey of Santa Lucia in Rome and presented to the Athenian priests on December 18, 1998. Other relics in the church include the bones of Tarcisius of Rome, Luke of Sympheroupolis, Marinus of Rab, Eutuxios of Sebastopol, and the Apostles Thomas and Peter. Personal communication from Father Demetrios Maroulis, Saint Philip's Church, Athens, email, January 25, 2013. I wish to thank Sylvie Dumont, Registrar of the Agora Excavations, and Bryn Mawr College graduate alumnae Dr. Johanna Best and Dr. Stella Diakou for their assistance in garnering information about the modern Basilica of Saint Philip in Athens.

IV

CONCLUSIONS

By the end of the War of Independence in 1832, the Greeks had recovered Athens—and its monuments—for themselves. After two millennia, the Tower's existence as a functional building came to an end, a longevity that renders it nearly unique among classical monuments.[1] The Octagon had performed diverse roles in the various historical periods—as a classical civic structure with cultic and commemorative functions, as a Christian martyrium, and as a Muslim lodge.

In review, the proposed chronology for and functions of the Tower of the Winds, as has been put forward herein, is as follows:

Circa 140–87/6 BC

The Horologion, built ca. 140 BC, with vertical sundials, a sculptured frieze depicting eight wind gods, and a weather vane in the form of a Triton on the exterior, contains a water-run mechanism inside—the display possibly comprising an astronomical device such as an orrery with a boat-shaped feature. It is also a cult site for the wind gods and may commemorate Boreas' role in Athenian victories during the Greco-Persian Wars. Architectural and other features in the interior include a central aperture in the floor, three freestanding columns on the south side, post-and-chain barriers around the apparatus and the periphery of the walls in the main chamber, and a closed water-powered system in the annex consisting of pipes and a holding tank. Both bi-leaf doors are opened to provide light and air. The northwest door is generally blocked by the post-and-chain barrier, directing access primarily through the northeast door. The ceiling is painted a deep blue and is adorned with depictions of astronomical and astrological figures. Attalos II of Pergamon is the likely patron who supplied funds for construction.

1. Other buildings that continued in use over many centuries include the Parthenon and the Temple of Hephaestus in Athens and the Temple of Athena in Syracuse. Only the Syracusan building continues, after two and a half millennia, to perform a religious function—as the cathedral of the city dedicated to the Virgin Mary (as was the Christian Parthenon).

Circa 86–84 BC

After the attack on Athens by Sulla, the interior mechanism, the bronze Triton weather vane, and the bronze gnomons from the sundials are possibly looted by the Romans.

Remainder of the First Century BC

The building is in private hands. The windowless empty chamber perhaps serves as a storehouse. The Roman writers, Vitruvius and Varro, both of whom may have visited the monument in person, mention the Tower in their commentaries. They focus on the number of the winds, and Andronikos of Kyrrhos is identified as the architect. No description of the interior and its mechanism is offered.

Roman Repairs (First Century AD)

The building is reclaimed for public ownership and restored to its original function. A low access door from the main chamber into the annex is created. A water-pipe channel is carved into the floor between the annex and the main chamber to facilitate the installation of a new water-run device. The water comes to the building aboveground via an aqueduct whose channel is supported by the arcuated wall on the south side of the annex.

Late Antiquity

The Roman mechanism is no longer extant (possibly it no longer functioned due to the lack of necessary maintenance or was destroyed or stolen during a foreign invasion). The wall around the small doorway to the annex is damaged, perhaps during looting of components of the mechanism.

Early Seventh Century through the Third Quarter of the Seventeenth Century

The building is converted by Christians into a commemorative church, or *memoria martyrum,* for the Apostle Philip. Any pagan religious paraphernalia on-site are removed. Latin crosses are carved into the exterior and interior wall surfaces; "Maltese" crosses are carved into the frame of the northwest door. A single-leaf door may have been installed at this time in the northeast porch. Byzantine paintings, which include an angel and a saint on horseback, are applied to the interior walls of the main chamber. A marble balustrade is installed that encircles the area where the small casket or reliquary stands at the center of the octagonal chamber. The three columns are incorporated for an unknown length of time into the circle of the balustrade. After the Ottoman conquest in the mid-fifteenth century, Muslim scholars use the building or the open area in front of it as a meeting place.

End of the Seventeenth Century through the First Decades of the Eighteenth Century

At some point between the Ottoman-Venetian War and the reconstruction of the city, the northeast entablature, a northeast porch column, the porch capitals, the upper courses of the annex, sections of the balustrade, and the three columns from the interior chamber are removed. Some or all of these objects are possibly taken to be reused elsewhere in rebuilding the city. The status of Saint Philip's relics is unknown.

Between 1735 and 1749

The Tower becomes the property of the Mevlevi sect of Sufi Islam, who convert it into a dervish lodge. The building, filled with soil and debris up to the first cornice, has a wood floor installed at this level for their dancing. A wood turban is placed as a finial atop the roof, signifying that the building had contained a burial.

1751

Stuart and Revett receive permission to excavate the monument. They clear several meters of soil and debris, exposing the exterior foundations and the interior marble floor. Several human bones are discovered in the fill. The building's architecture and sculpture are documented in detail. Upon completion of the work, the Tower is returned to the Mevlevis.

1752

Fill is reintroduced into the Octagon, and a new wood floor is laid at the level of the first cornice of the main chamber to accommodate the dervish dance. A viewing balcony is built on the upper west wall. A mihrab is built into the inner face of the southeast wall and contains a Quran. Plaques displaying Quranic verses and other items of Islamic worship are installed. A block from the northwest wall is removed to allow light to fall on the mihrab. A block from the north wall is removed, which allows light to fall on the south wall. A plaster turban replaces the wood turban as the finial on the roof. The northeast lintel is painted red and carries the first pillar of Islam: "There is no God but God and Muhammad is his prophet."

Second Half of the Eighteenth Century

The cult of Saint Philip is housed in a basilica consecrated in his name that is built on the site north of the Greek Agora, where tradition says the apostle preached while living in Athens.

Early Nineteenth Century

Dervish rituals and renovations to the Octagon are documented by a number of European travelers. The Greek War for Independence breaks out in 1821. At its end in 1832, with the Greeks victorious, the Turks leave Athens. The Tower is no longer functional. It will become an archaeological site.

Among the various hypotheses that have been put forward, four can be considered to be primary: the relative and absolute chronologies for certain architectural features within the building, the identity of the patron who financed construction of the Octagon, the cultic and commemorative classification of the monument, and the identity of the Christian martyr.

Different chronological phases are proposed for specific architectural elements from the interior that have all generally been considered as part of the original phase of construction in the Hellenistic period. These include three freestanding columns on the south side of the main chamber, two series of small holes that encircle the central area and the outer edge of the floor, and the balustrade. The quality of the workmanship and the precision with which these features relate to the architectural plan are evidence that the freestanding columns are the only elements that are part of the Hellenistic design. The two series of small holes were added somewhat later. The balustrade was installed during the Christian renovations.

Several factors speak in favor of Attalos II as the Tower's most likely patron. These include the epigraphic evidence attesting to the long history of Attalid support for the city from the beginning of the second century BC until the end of the Pergamene dynasty, the numerous monuments in second-century Athens donated by Pergamene kings, the great respect for and support of the culture and educational institutions of Athens by members of the royal family, parallels in stylistic details between sculpture from the Pergamon Altar and on the Tower, and similarities between the letter forms in the inscription on the Stoa of Attalos and in the names of the wind gods on the Octagon.

Defining the Horologion as a cultic and commemorative monument, along with its meteorological and chronometric functions (weather vane and sundials), derives first from analysis of its architectural typology. Buildings belonging to this classification can be found in Asia Minor and elsewhere in the Greek world beginning in the mid-fourth century BC and continuing throughout the Hellenistic period. These are tall centralized structures with some form of colonnade at the upper level, characteristics shared by the Tower. The most prominent feature on the exterior of the Horologion is the large frieze depicting the eight wind gods. Boreas is the focal point of the reliefs, for he is in the most prominent position on the edifice. The North Wind was a very important figure in the mythic history of Athens as the son-in-law of a legendary king. He was even more important, however, in the actual history of the city as a result of the part he played in the victory of the Greeks over the Persian Navy.

Whether the relics entombed in the Tower belonged to the Apostle Philip cannot be determined with assuredness, although the data support a strong argument in favor of this hypothesis. They include the following.

1. The closed balustrade in the main chamber, which would have prohibited access to the area within, leads to the conclusion that the Christian function of the building was as a martyrium rather than as a church or baptistery, both of which would have required a point of entry for access to either the altar or the baptismal font.

2. The size, elegance, and location of the Octagon suggest that it was the martyrium of an individual who, at the least, should be among the saints listed in church calendars and other religious documents.

3. The Turkish traveler Evliya, who inspected the interior of the Tower in 1668, says that it was the burial site of a Christian saint and that the name "Philip" was written in Greek on the casket.

4. Saints named Philip—from Sicily, Crete, and Thrace—seem to have had no connection with Athens. On the other hand, for Christians in Late Antiquity when the Tower was converted from pagan use, the Apostle Philip was considered to be an important figure in the early Christian history of the city. His two-year sojourn in Athens, during which he preached and founded a congregation, is related in the non-canonical *Acts of Philip*.

5. Historical and archaeological evidence inform us that the apostle's remains were originally interred in Hierapolis in Asia Minor. After the destruction of his martyrium there in the sixth century, the bones were translated to Constantinople and Rome. A small number of bones may also have been sent to Athens, in a manner similar to the dispersal at the time of numerous saints' relics from the Holy Lands and Constantinople to churches of all sizes across the Christian world.

6. In assessing why relics of a notable New Testament figure would go unmentioned in the historical record, one must take into consideration that documents from the

period following Late Antiquity are neither numerous nor very informative. Among comments relating to Christian monuments, the cult of Mary and the great Parthenon cathedral overshadow all other religious figures and sites in Athens.

7. At some point after the Mevlevi Muslims took ownership of the Tower, a basilica named in honor of the apostle was built on the site where, as described in the *Acts of Philip,* he preached, thus demonstrating that the chronicle of Philip's stay in Athens seems to have been preserved down the centuries along with a desire to maintain a place for his veneration.

When reflecting upon the long yet finite history of this monument as discussed herein—as a horologion, planetarium, polytheistic cultic and commemorative monument, storehouse, Christian martyrium, and Muslim dervish lodge—a statement by the sixth-century Christian philosopher Boethius in *The Consolation of Philosophy* (Book II, Meter III)comes to mind:

> When Zephyr's gentle breath warms the springtime, roses bud. But a sudden storm from the south can strip the bushes to bare thorns. The sea, sometimes serene, glints a pale and unruffled blue, but the North Wind assails it, and the storms rage and the sea churns. The beauty of earth changes. Enjoy it but never think to trust it. As with the fleeting pleasures of men, a stern law decrees that nothing in life lasts." (trans. D. R. Slavitt).

APPENDICES

The following appendices present an overview of Christian buildings constructed in Athens in Late Antiquity and classical buildings (in Athens and elsewhere) that were converted to Christian use during the same period. This synopsis is intended to provide supplementary context into which can be placed the Hellenistic and Roman Tower of the Winds as converted into a Christian martyrium.

Appendix 1

The First Christian Churches in Athens

To the degree that can be determined, Athenian Christians worshipped in private houses for the first several hundred years following the founding of the religion. Thus, the number of early churches constitutes a small population of edifices within the city walls. For the fifth and sixth centuries, excavations and literary evidence attest to the existence of fewer than two dozen structures that can be identified as churches. This is likely to be an incomplete listing of the original number, since a good many sculptured architectural fragments dating to this period—and clearly coming from Christian buildings—have been found reused in later structures. Much of this material cannot be connected to buildings in or near the city center, so the original contexts likely were basilicas located in the outskirts of Athens that were destroyed in the invasions of the Slavs and Avars.[1]

It was more common for Athenian Christians to construct new church buildings than to restore and renovate ancient temples and other classical monuments. Many

1. Frantz identifies fourteen Early Christian churches, while Castrén thinks there were twenty-two churches in Athens and its outskirts (including the Parthenon and the Tetraconch in the ""Library of Hadrian");" see Frantz (1965) 187–88, 194–95; Frantz (1988) 72 and n. 105; Hanson (1978) 265–66; Castrén (1999) 222–23; Kiilerich (2013) 187–214. The earliest churches in the Peloponnese were, likewise, built in the suburbs of cities; see Sweetman (2015) passim, esp. 512.

of these early basilicas, as mentioned above, were built on the periphery of Athens, especially in the area to the southeast. Along with the fact that the center of the city was controlled by polytheists for much of Late Antiquity, these decisions were effected by two factors arising from the various invasions: many classical buildings were ruined and unusable, and Athens was greatly reduced in size, resulting in a paucity of land available for construction within the contracted city.

The earliest identifiable church in Athens and possibly its first cathedral was the tetraconch building that was constructed inside the courtyard of the so-called Library of Hadrian, a large second-century complex to the north of the Roman Agora. This Hadrianic forum housed a sanctuary for the Imperial cult as well as a library and may also have been the repository for public documents recording land values and real estate taxes (the cadastral archives). Although much of this building complex was severely damaged in the Herulian invasion, it had been restored by the beginning of the fifth century. The tetraconch church was constructed shortly afterward (probably in the second quarter of the fifth century); thus, the Imperial cult must have ceased to exist by that time, and its altars must have been removed, for it would not have been acceptable for pagan and Christian religious accoutrements to occupy the same space. The size of the tetraconch building and its location in the city center are indicative of the increasing growth and influence of the Christian community at this time. Destroyed by fire in the Slavic siege of the sixth century, the church was rebuilt in the seventh century as a three-aisled basilica. As a result of the economic devastation of Athens wrought by the siege, however, the new structure was smaller and of far poorer quality than its predecessor. Nearby within the open area of the Roman Agora, another three-aisled basilica, also dating to the seventh century, was constructed.[2]

The theater in the Sanctuary of Dionysus, one of the most important civic buildings in classical Athens, was the site of the first performances of many of the great fifth-century BC dramas that have survived antiquity. Renovated on several occasions during the Greek and Roman periods, it served over time as well for gladiatorial combats and, more important, for meetings of the Athenian citizen assembly. The theater—along with the Santuary of Asclepius, the Odeum of Pericles, the Odeum of Herodes Atticus, and other monuments on the south slope of the Acropolis—was heavily damaged in the Herulian invasion. Repairs were carried out at some point in the fourth century. By the early sixth century after the theater had fallen out of use, a one-aisled basilica was built in the east *parodos*, with the orchestra serving as its courtyard.[3]

The healing sanctuary of Asclepius (Paus. 1.21.7), adjacent to the theater, after suffering damage was also restored and continued in use by polytheists during the fourth and fifth centuries. By the sixth century its temple had been razed to the foundations, and a

2. Frantz (1988) 72–73; Karivieri (1994) 89 and nn. 2–3, 102 and n. 91, 103 and n. 93, 106–08, 112–13, figs. 4a and 4b; Castrén (1994) 2–4, 12; Castrén (1999) 211.

3. Frantz (1965) 196; Frantz (1988) 34–39; Travlos (1971) 538, fig. 686 (VIII); Sironen (1994) 43–45; Castrén (1999) 216; Goette (2001) 50–52.

sizable three-aisled basilica dedicated to the Impoverished Saints (Aghioi Anargyroi), the physicians Cosmas and Damian, was built atop the ruins largely from the earlier building's architectural remains. This Christian sanctuary incorporated several of the classical sanctuary's elements for its healing rituals, including the pagan incubation stoa and what may have been an inn (*katagogeion*) for visiting pilgrims. In spite of the fact that the pagan temple was demolished and votive stelai honoring Asclepius were defaced, it has been suggested that the reuse of these and other architectural structures in the Sanctuary of Asclepius is an indication of the integration of the pagan healing sanctuary with the Christian healing sanctuary.[4]

On the outskirts of the city, the area southeast of the Acropolis near the Ilissus River was the site of many classical shrines and temples. The largest of these was the colossal Temple of Olympian Zeus. Its precinct wall began to be dismantled in the mid-third century when a number of its blocks were employed in the construction of the Valerian Wall (AD 253–260, the predecessor of the Post-Herulian Wall). The temple, however, remained in use until at least the mid-fifth century. By the sixth century, the great building began to fall into ruin. A large three-aisled basilica, whose walls were adorned with coffers from the temple's ceiling, was constructed in the area of the pronaos between the remains of the peribolos wall and an adjacent second-century Roman bath.[5]

To the southeast of the Temple of Olympian Zeus, the Roman Temple of Cronus and Rhea (Pausanias 1.18.7) shared a similar history. The architectural members of the small Doric monument (built ca. AD 150) were dismantled for use in construction of the Post-Herulian Wall, and the site remained unused until the sixth century, at which time a church was built atop the rubble.[6]

These and other basilicas constructed in the fifth and sixth centuries on the periphery of Athens were all destroyed in the Slavic siege of AD 580 and never rebuilt, with one exception: a three-aisled basilica from the fifth century that stood on the bank of the Ilissus River. This edifice is believed to have been the second church building to be constructed by the local Christian community, following the tetraconch church in the "Library of Hadrian".[7]

4. Frantz (1965) 194–95; Travlos (1971) 127–28, fig. 172; Gregory (1986) 237–39, nn. 31–36; Castrén (1999) 221 and n. 44; Goette (2001) 49–50; Hurwit (2004) 218–23.; Lefantzis and Tae Jensen (2009) 91–124
5. Travlos (1971) 403, fig. 380 (no. 158).
6. Travlos (1971) 335, 403, figs. 379 (no. 159), 380 (no. 159), 437–440; Wycherley (1978) 164–65; Frantz (1988) 73 and nn. 109–115.
7. Frantz (1965) 204–05 and n. 102; Frantz (1988) 73; Camp (2001) 235.

Appendix 2

The Conversion of Classical Structures in Athens for Christian Use

It may seem surprising that among the city's many classical buildings only a small number were adapted to Christian use between the fifth and seventh centuries, but one must remember, as stated above, that numerous Athenian edifices were severely damaged or destroyed in various foreign invasions and thus were no longer available for occupation. With so few existing pagan buildings available for re-consecration as Christian churches or shrines, the limited inventory by necessity consists of various types of structures—religious and secular, from large temples to small caves. They were located, with two exceptions, within the Post-Herulian Wall, primarily on the top and the slopes of the Acropolis.

Of the many pagan temples that at one time adorned Athens, only four were converted to Christian churches: the city's three most renowned classical religious buildings—the Parthenon, the Erechtheum, the Temple of Hephaestus—and a small temple on the Ilissus River. The fact that they were converted into Christian churches is a major contributor to why they survived to their full height into the modern era. No evidence exists to support the conversion of a classical temple to a church before the sixth century. The Parthenon was likely converted in the late sixth century.[1] The Erechtheum, the Temple of Hephaestus, and the Ilissus temple were probably Christianized in the seventh century.

The Parthenon and the Propylaea

The most famous classical building in Athens—and indeed in all the Christian world—that was transformed into a church was the Parthenon. This and other Greek temples functioned in antiquity quite differently from Christian churches. Most notably, the primary pagan ritual—sacrifice attended by religious officials and worshippers—took place at an altar outside the temple's main entrance, which (with a few exceptions) was on the east. The building's main purpose was usually to house a statue of the

1. Frantz (1988) 92. Mango (1995) 203, posits, however, that the Parthenon became a church in the second half of the fifth century when the colossal cult statue was removed.

deity as well as precious offerings to it. Conversely, Christian churches were entered from the west. The altars, priests, and congregants were disposed inside the edifice, and the rituals took place there. Of course, precious offerings were also placed inside churches.

The huge mid-fifth-century BC Doric temple, the central focus of the Periclean reconstruction program on the Acropolis in which monuments destroyed during the Greco-Persian Wars were built anew, was dedicated in 432 BC to Athena Parthenos. It is a large peripteral building of Pentelic marble with eight columns across the ends and seventeen along the sides. A shallow hexastyle prostyle pronaos on the east led through massive doors into a rectangular cella with U-shaped two-storey Doric colonnades (ten by five) on the north, west, and south sides. Near the western columns stood the great gold and ivory statue fashioned by Pheidias. On the building's west end, a shallow hexastyle prostyle porch led into a large nearly square chamber whose roof was supported by four Ionic or, possibly, Corinthian columns.[2] The exterior of the Parthenon was more heavily adorned with architectural sculpture than any other Greek temple. Its east pediment bore the birth of Athena. On the west was the battle with her uncle Poseidon for possession of Athens. Ninety-two sculptured metopes ornamented the four sides, portraying a Gigantomachy (east), the Sack of Troy (north), an Amazonomachy (west), and a Centauromachy (south). Within the peristyle around the upper exterior walls and encircling the pronaos, the cella, and the west porch was a frieze, ca. 160 meters in length, that depicted a procession moving toward a gathering of deities on the east side.

At some point in the third or fourth century, the temple experienced a serious fire that resulted in severe damage to the pediments, the entablatures, the east and west doors, the columns on the exterior and interior, the walls, and the wood elements of the roof, which collapsed. It is not known whether the conflagration was the result of an accident or occurred during one of the foreign invasions. The great building was repaired in the fourth or fifth century (unfortunately, no written records are extant that tell us when or by whom), but it was not returned to its former elegance. Interior colonnades were constructed using columns that were removed from one or more of the city's damaged stoas. The roof was of terracotta tiles rather than marble. It covered only the chambers of the temple, leaving the peristyle open to the sky.[3]

No textual evidence exists describing precisely when, why, or by whom the Parthenon was converted into a Christian church. Ward-Perkins cogently suggests that pragmatic forces were at work.[4] The city had been devastated by the Slavic invasions, and there were few funds available for rebuilding. The Parthenon was in serviceable condition

2. Goette (2001) 32–39; Hurwit (2004) 106–54; Connelly (2014) 93 and n. 53; 234 and nn. 87 and 88; fig. on page 233.
3. Korres (1996) 140–46; Hurwit (1999) 285–86 and nn. 12 and 13; Ousterhout (2005) 298–322; Kaldellis (2009) 23–31. Hurwit makes a strong case for the damage having been caused by the Herulians and repairs having been carried out in the fourth century.
4. Ward-Perkins (1999) 225–44, esp. 233–40.

and was a massive structure. It was thus appropriate for conversion into the city's cathedral. Also, it was on the Acropolis, the most secure site in Athens.

Fortunately, the archaeological evidence does inform us as to how the alterations were accomplished.[5] As with other converted temples, the orientation of the building was reversed, with the main entrance transferred to the west porch. The spaces between the columns of the now roofless peristyle were closed by high screen walls through which a number of doors gave access to this ambulatory. The columns of the west porch were also joined by screen walls in order to create an enclosed space that served as an exonarthex. The west chamber of the Parthenon became the narthex of the church. A baptistery, separated by screen walls, was built into its northwest corner.

Three doors in the farther wall of the narthex led into the old cella, now the nave, which was given the form of a three-aisled basilica divided by the extant interior colonnades. The center column of the west colonnade was removed to provide direct access from the west entrance through the narthex into the nave. A gallery was created in the nave by placing a wood floor between the upper level of the two-storey colonnade and the lateral walls. Three windows were opened in the upper lateral walls to supply more light. A marble pulpit of curved marble panels adorned with crosses in relief stood in the nave, which was separated from the sanctuary area by a low wall (chancel screen) consisting of sculptured marble panels alternating with short columns. The main altar stood here beneath a canopy (*ciborium*) supported by four porphyry pillars.

The temple's original entrance in the east wall was closed, and an apse with a raised floor was built in its place. Inside the apse was a raised curved platform (*synthronon*) on which stood chairs for priests on either side of the bishop's throne (a sculptured marble chair dating to the classical period, perhaps removed from the Theater of Dionysus).

During Christian renovations, a good amount of damage occurred, both from necessity and choice, to the architectural sculpture on the Parthenon, especially to the center of the east pediment. The metopes on the east, west, and north sides were deliberately defaced. But a significant portion of the figural adornment was left intact and in place on this and the other converted Athenian temples. The Centauromachy depicted in the south metopes, for example, was left essentially untouched. This may have been due to their location on the south side of the building, which was away from the usual path visitors would follow, and thus the reliefs may have been infrequently seen.[6] While it may seem an odd choice by Christian authorities to retain any classical sculpture depicting mythological themes at the time when temples were converted into churches, this practice was permitted under the Theodosian Code (XVI 10.8, 15, 18) as long as the structure was not used for pagan purposes. It is also true for this particular building that a great deal of sculpture was integrally tied to various architectural members of the edifice, and thus it would have been difficult to remove.

5. Travlos (1971) figs. 576–578; Hurwit (1999) 293–95; Connelly (2014) fig. on page 337.
6. Hurwit (1999) 171.

At the time of the conversion of the Parthenon, part of the great gateway to the Acropolis—the Propylaea—was also called into Christian service. Its southern chamber was renovated to serve as a chapel in the form of a one-aisled basilica. A variety of major changes were made over the centuries to this monumental gateway to the Acropolis. In the middle Byzantine period (ninth century through the beginning of the thirteenth century), a residence for the Orthodox archbishop was built into the building's north section by enclosing the spaces between the columns and inserting a floor to create a two-storey structure.[7]

In the early thirteenth century when soldiers of the Fourth Crusade attacked Athens, the metropolitan archbishop Michael Choniates chose to surrender the city rather than allow it to be sacked. For the next 250 years (1208–1458), Athens was under the rule of a series of Latin dukes. The first, a Burgundian named Othon de la Roche, installed a French archbishop in the Parthenon cathedral, which was now called Notre Dame d'Athènes. The Frankish dukes were followed by Catalans (in 1311) and finally by the Acciaiuoli family of Florence (in 1388). During this period of Latin rule, the only modification to the church was a tower (with an interior spiral staircase) built into the southeast corner of the exonarthex. Whether this was a watchtower or a belfry is not known.[8] The Propylaea, however, underwent significant reconstruction, especially in regard to enlarging and fortifying the edifice as a ducal palace. Also, a one-aisled basilica dedicated to Saint Bartholomew was constructed on the building's north side.[9]

Between 1456 and 1458, the Ottoman Turks laid siege to Athens. After their victory, the Acropolis became their fortress and the Propylaea palace was the residence of the military commander; as such, access for the public was restricted. Shortly after the Muslim conquest of the city, the Parthenon became a mosque that, according to sixteenth-century tax records, was called the Mosque of Athens or the Mosque of the Castle of Athens.[10] Again, there is no written account of the alterations carried out, and one must rely on archaeological evidence. Few modifications, however, appear to have been required for the conversion. The Tower in the exonarthex was rebuilt as a minaret. The altars and chancel screen were removed. A mihrab was built to the right of the apse; a pulpit (*minbar*) stood to the left. The *ciborium* and *synthronon* remained in place, as did much of the classical sculpture on the exterior of the building. A mosaic in the apse depicting the Virgin Mary was not covered by a layer of whitewash, in contrast to the Christian frescoes adorning the walls.[11] Over time, the windows were blocked.

7. Tanoulas (1994) 56, 58.
8. Korres (1994) 49; Hurwit (1999) 291; Goette (2001) 17–21; Hurwit (2004) 155–63; Ousterhout (2005) 314–16 and nn. 122, 128.
9. Tanoulas (1994) 60–65.
10. D'Ooge (1908) 317; Hurwit (1999) 295; Ousterhout (2005) 320 and n. 151.
11. For discussion of the Byzantine wall paintings in the Parthenon, see Cutler (1993–1994) 171–80.

After the end of the Turkish-Venetian Wars of the late seventeenth century, the Parthenon, along with the rest of the city, was in ruins. At some point after the Acropolis fortifications were repaired in 1708, a small, square, poorly constructed domed mosque with no minaret was built on a northwest-southeast axis inside the remains of the temple peristyle (Ill. 43).

The Erechtheum

The Erechtheum, to the north of the Parthenon on the Acropolis, also underwent several incarnations throughout its long history—as a classical temple, a Christian basilica consecrated to the Virgin Mary, an annex to the Propylaea palace, and a Turkish residence.[12] Surprisingly, written accounts by Babin, Guillet, and other Renaissance visitors to Athens do not mention the Erechtheum. Those who went up to the Acropolis seemed to have focused their attention primarily—or solely—on the Parthenon.

The Erechtheum, built in the last quarter of the fifth century BC, was not a typical rectangular peripteral temple honoring a single deity. The Ionic building is divided into two main sections separated by a cross-wall. Facing east is a hexastyle pronaos whose door opens into a cella dedicated to Athena Polias (Paus. 1.16.7). Facing west are two chambers side by side, with a forecourt whose access is through an elaborate porch on the north. The western half of the temple housed several cults honoring Poseidon, Hephaestus, the hero Boutes, and others as well as the tombs of the mythic kings Erechtheus and Cecrops. On the building's southwest corner is the ornate Porch of the Caryatids.

When the temple was reconfigured to serve as a Christian church, probably in the seventh century, the north porch became the main entrance. This led into the forecourt, which became the narthex. Three doors in its east wall gave access to a nave with two aisles created by removing all the walls separating the cella and the smaller adjacent chambers. Dividing the nave from the aisles were colonnades of dark green marble, the columns of which were probably reused from the Roman reconstruction of the Erechtheum or from another Roman building. Four windows were opened in the upper lateral walls to provide more light. The floor of the nave was paved with thin marble slabs, while the aisle floors were beaten earth.[13] The entrance on the east end, to what had been the cella, was closed and rebuilt with an apse separated from the nave by an iconostasis. Rooms at the east ends of the aisles served as the *prothesis* (north) and *diaconicon* (south).

There is no clear evidence as to the status of the Erechtheum during the period when the Latin dukes ruled Athens. The building seems to have served as an annex to the pal-

12. Paton (1927) passim, esp. 492–93, 510–19 and n. 6, 529; Goette (2001), 25–29, fig. 10; Hurwit (2004) 164–80.

13. The same system of flooring was found in a Byzantine church at Olympia; see Paton (1927) 499, 501 and n. 2.

ace in the Propylaea, however, and may have been entirely secular. After the Ottoman Turks conquered Athens in 1458 and the Acropolis became a fortress for their military garrison, the Erechtheum was used as a residence for a Turkish man whose name has not come down to us.[14] There is little evidence regarding any additional reconstruction being carried out at this time with two exceptions: the Caryatid porch was enclosed by walling up the spaces between the sculptured figures, and cisterns were built beneath the floors of the north porch and the narthex area of the church.

The Temple of Hephaestus

The mid-fifth-century BC temple dedicated to Hephaestus (Paus. 1.14.5), on a low hill to the west of the Greek Agora, remains one of the best-preserved Greek monuments from antiquity. It is a Doric building of Pentelic marble oriented east to west with a canonical peristyle of six by thirteen columns.[15] The classical edifice had a deep distyle-in-antis pronaos; a long rectangular cella may have contained U-shaped two-storey Doric colonnades (five by three columns) on the north, west, and south;[16] and a distyle-in-antis opisthodomos. The building was adorned with a significant amount of architectural sculpture.[17]

The Temple of Hephaestus was reconfigured as a church dedicated to Saint George at approximately the same time as the conversion of the Erechtheum, in the seventh century AD. In its primary phase of reconstruction, a number of changes were required. At the west end, the opisthodomos became the narthex. A door was opened in the wall dividing the opisthodomos from the cella, which became a one-aisled nave. The interior colonnades, which stood close to the lateral walls, were left in place except for the central column on the west, which was removed to allow direct access from the door through the nave. A round apse was created on the east end by removing the two pronaos columns and most of the wall separating the cella from the pronaos. A second phase of reconstruction occurred at some point in the middle Byzantine period that included removal of the interior colonnades and roofing the entire nave (the area of the

14. Paton (1927) 528, says the oft-repeated tale that it housed the harem of the Turkish governor is not supported by the evidence.
15. Dinsmoor (1975) 179–81, fig. 67.
16. It has been suggested bronze statues of Hephaistos and Athena, possibly by Alkamenes, stood on a base at the west end of the cella; see Barringer (2009) 107, 109 and n. 16, fig. 10.13.
17. Ridgway (1981) 26–30, 85–88; Barringer (2009) passim, esp. 105–20, figs. 10.3, 4, 5a, 5b, 7, 8, 9. The figured pediments are in fragmentary condition and the themes have not been identified, although Barringer suggests the center of the east pediment may have contained a seated Hephaistos with a standing Athena. Eighteen figured metopes adorned the east end of the temple—ten on the façade depicting the labors of Heracles, and four each on the northeast and southeast corners showing the deeds of Theseus. Extending across the entire width of the pronaos was a continuous frieze portraying Theseus in combat; the identity of his opponents is unclear. In the opisthodomos, a second continuous frieze, spanning the space between the antae, displays a Centauromachy.

cella and the pronaos) with a barrel vault. A polygonal apse replaced the round apse.[18] Apparently an unsuccessful attempt to convert the Christian Temple of Hephaestus (the Church of Saint George) into a mosque was made in the seventeenth century, for according to Kyriakos Pittakis: "In 1660 the Turks had begun to destroy this temple to make a mosque; the Greeks prevented it by presenting an order which had arrived from Constantinople."[19]

The Ilissus Temple

On a low hill above the south bank of the Ilissus River stood a small Ionic temple very similar in form to the Temple of Athena Nike at the west end of the Acropolis. Both were constructed at about the same time (ca. 430 BC). The Ilissus temple was tetrastyle amphiprostyle with a deep pronaos, a square cella, and no opisthodomos.[20] It was adorned with a sculptured continuous frieze of which only a few fragments are extant; consequently, its theme remains unidentified. The building was converted into a church dedicated to Saint Mary on the Rock in the mid-fifth century and survived as a church nearly intact until it was demolished in the latter eighteenth century, either so its Pentelic marble blocks could be used in the construction of a new city wall or to build a new church elsewhere. Fortunately, it was among the monuments studied and recorded by Stuart and Revett. When the classical temple was converted by Christian architects, the orientation was reversed by cutting a door into the rear (west) wall of the cella, now the narthex. A domed roof was built above this chamber. In creating a nave, the two central columns of the east colonnade and the two distyle-in-antis piers of the pronaos were removed. A deep round apse extended beyond the area of the pronaos. The nave and apse were covered by a low curved roof.

Other Converted Classical Monuments

Within the confines of the Post-Herulian Wall was a small number of classical secular buildings and minor religious monuments converted in Late Antiquity to serve as places for Christian worship. The largest of these is the building commonly and erroneously identified as the headquarters of the market officials (the *agoranomoi*) that stands immediately southeast of the Horologion and encroaches on the lowest step of its *crepidoma.* The edifice, dating to the mid-first century AD, may not have been a

18. Orlandos (1936) 207–16; Dinsmoor (1941) 6–15; Travlos (1971) 262, fig. 335 (below).
19. Pittakiés (1835) 87.
20. Stuart and Revett (1762), chapter 2, pl. 2; Stuart and Revett (1825), chapter 2, pls. 7–11; Miles (1980) 311 and n. 14, 319, fig. 1. According to Travlos (1971) 112–13, figs. 154 (no. 151), 156, 159, 379 (no. 151), this temple was dedicated to Artemis Agrotera (the Huntress).

civic structure but may have housed the Imperial cult in the Julio-Claudian period.[21] Carved into the walls of the "Agoranomion" are several Christian symbols, leading Orlandos, Frantz, and others to conclude that it was converted into a church.

On the south slope of the Acropolis, to the north of the Sanctuary of Asclepius, is a natural cave in the native rock that contains a sacred spring, which was used in the worship of the healing god. The cave was transformed into a Christian chapel, very likely at the time when a basilica was built on the foundations of the pagan temple. The façade, reconstructed with an arched doorway, opened into the cave, which was refashioned as a circular domed chamber. A painting of the Virgin Mary still adorns the rear wall above the spring.[22]

On the top tier of the *cavea* of the Theater of Dionysus is a small late fourth-century BC monument commemorating a man named Thrasyllos. Its three-stepped flat roof originally supported the bronze tripod he was awarded for his victory in a choragic competition. The façade has three doors, separated by Doric pilasters, opening into a small chamber constructed within a natural cave. Pausanias (1.21.4–5), in what appears to be a description of this monument, states that the interior contained a display (whether sculptured or painted is not recorded) depicting Apollo and Artemis slaying the children of Niobe. The pagan monument was converted with few alterations into a Christian chapel dedicated to the Virgin Mary, called Our Lady of the Cave (Panaghia Spilaiotissa).[23]

On the north slope of the Acropolis, an area comprising caves and unroofed shrines was dedicated after the Greco-Persian Wars to the Greek deity Pan. The main part of the cult site, an open area with votive niches carved into the cliff face, was adapted into a Christian shrine generally believed to have been dedicated to Saint Athanasios. A faded fresco still displays his image.[24]

In summary, the following comments by Ousterhout clearly define the practice of the conversion of pagan monuments in Athens to Christian use. While he specifically addresses the reuse of temples, his observations are applicable to all types of architecture.

> The detailed analysis of the archaeological evidence suggests that rather than attributable to aesthetic motivation or symbolic appropriation, the decision to reuse temple sites for Christian worship came out of necessity, as part of urban retrenchment.... [It] did not represent a powerful symbolic act, a "triumph" of Christianity over paganism, but rather a cautious and relatively late change in thinking inspired by the straited circumstances at the end of antiquity.[25]

---

21. Orlandos (1964) 58–59; Travlos (1971) 37; Frantz (1988) 71; Hoff (1994) passim, esp. 97–99. Travlos suggests that the actual Agoranomion was most likely near the west gate of the Roman Agora.
22. D'Ooge (1908) 252, figs. 110 and 111; Plan VI, no. 1.
23. Welter (1938) 34–67, esp. 34–35; Goette (2001) 52–53, fig. 17.
24. Travlos (1971) 417, figs. 116, 536, says it is in honor of the third century saint Athanasios; Goette (2001) 54, names the honoree as the fourth century saint John Chrysostom.
25. Ousterhout (2005) 301.

Appendix 3

The Conversion of Classical Heroa into Christian Martyria

The gods honored in the reliefs of the Tower of the Winds were of significantly lower status in the pantheon than the great Olympian divinities. These chthonic deities were instead worshipped in a fashion similar to Greek heroes. The process by which the Tower was transformed from a cult site for Greek gods into a saint's martyrium was different from the conversions of the two heroa described below in that it did not include the evolution of a pagan cult directly into a Christian cult. Evidence supplied by the excavations of these heroa at Philippi (in northeastern Greece) and the Cycladic island Sikinos, however, demonstrates that reuse of cult sites for heroes and chthonic deities could be accomplished with relative facility.

The Heroon at Philippi

In the center of ancient Philippi south of a large Roman bath complex (*balneum*) are the remains of a Hellenistic heroon built ca. 150 BC.[1] Within its walled *temenos* was a *naiskos* oriented on a north-south axis that stood on a three-stepped platform (4.70 by 6 meters), with an entrance on the north façade. Beneath the remains of the *naiskos* is a barrel-vaulted chamber (similar to tombs in Macedonia), which was entered through a single-leaf door (found in situ) on the south side. On both the east and west walls of this underground chamber are two small niches; a single niche is cut into the north wall. An offering table (perhaps dating to the Christian period) stands near the northwest corner. In the center of the floor excavators discovered an intact cist grave, among the finds of which was a Macedonian-type diadem adorned with leaves of gold foil, gold appliqué ornaments from clothing, and other Hellenistic gold jewelry. On the lid of the cist was inscribed the name of the interred person: Euephenes, son of Exekestos (ΕΥΗΦΕΝΗΣ ΕΞΗΚΕΣΤΟΥ), whom the excavator describes as a youth, not an adult. Euephenes' name is found in several other inscriptions. In one from Philippi and another from Samothrace, he is described as an initiate into the mystery cult of the Great Gods. The names Euephenes and Exekestos are also found in inscriptions

1. Verhoef (2008) 697–714; Koukouli-Chrysanthaki and Bakirtzis (1995) 49–54, figs. 40–41, 43–47. The site was excavated by S. Pelekanidis between 1958–1982.

from Thasos. Since only founding heroes were accorded burial within Greek cities and because Philippi was founded by Thasians in 360 BC, it is postulated that these names belong to members of the founding family of Philippi.

In the first half of the fourth century, a relatively small Christian basilica named for Saint Paul the Apostle was built adjacent to the Hellenistic *temenos.* Philippi was the first European city visited by Paul (Acts 16:11–12), and thus he was especially venerated there. The heroon of Euephenes was left in place, with the south wall of the *naiskos* and its south *temenos* wall forming part of the north wall of the church. A door in this wall opened directly from the church onto the *naiskos* platform.

The basilica burned ca. AD 400 and was replaced shortly after by a larger octagonal church (which survived until the early seventh century). The heroon was again left in place but was now in the center of and completely surrounded by Christian structures. Added to the basilica at this time were chambers (several of which served the ritual of baptism) built to the west, north, and east of the heroon. Included were a room for instruction of initiates (catechumens); a dressing room (*apodyterion*); a room for confirmation and anointing (*chrismation*); a sacristy for vestments, books, etc. (*diaconicon*); a room for ecclesiastical implements (e.g., sacred vessels) and offerings, which also contained a small round cistern (*prothesis*); a chamber with a cruciform baptismal font; and a room containing a fountain that is hypothesized to have been part of a Byzantine water clock. Within the *diaconicon* was a rectangular marble basin (1.00 x 2.50 meters and 0.93 meters deep) covered by a *tegurium.* Even though water for the basin in the *diaconicon* and for the cistern in the *prothesis* flowed first through the *balneum,* it was considered to be holy once it left the public baths and entered the rooms attached to the Christian basilica. Bones found in the *diaconicon* are believed to be from a sarcophagus or reliquary that belonged to a saint; the excavators suggest that they may be those of the Apostle Paul.

The preservation of the classical heroon at Philippi and its integration into the Christian building complex are evidence that the cult continued throughout the Hellenistic and Roman periods to some point in the mid-fourth century, by which time the pagan hero had evolved into a Christian saint. Possibly one element that facilitated the transformation of Euephenes from a local hero into a local saint may have been the fact that the pagan cult honored an individual who was a worshipper of the Great Gods of Samothrace, deities who promised a blessed afterlife, a theological concept also central to Christianity.

The Heroon on Sikinos

A heroon on the Cycladic island Sikinos,[2] dating to the first half of the third century AD, seems to have followed a similar pattern of evolution although over a shorter period

2. Frantz, et al. (1969) passim.

of time. This well-preserved Doric-Ionic structure, of local marble, had a *naiskos* with a distyle-in-antis pronaos on a tall platform (oriented southwest-northeast) beneath which were two barrel-vaulted tomb chambers. An inscription on the right-hand door jamb of the *naiskos* describes the honoree as a woman with the wisdom of Athena and the beauty of Hera whom the gods have taken to spend eternity with famous women from the past. While it was not uncommon from the Hellenistic period onward for deceased males to be referred to as "hero" in inscriptions, such designation for a woman was rare. Unfortunately, the first line, which contained the heroine's name, is missing, cut away in the later Christian reconstruction. The building was converted into a church in the seventh century with a modicum of alterations. The original doors leading into the tomb chambers had been located in the platform wall but were heavily damaged in an earthquake shortly before the conversion of the heroon. The vaults, in which the excavators found human bones, not only were left intact by the Christian renovators but also were made accessible after the earthquake through openings created in the floor of the cella. There is no evidence of the vaults being used for some newly introduced Christian purpose. Instead, it seems that over several centuries this pagan heroine came to be seen as a woman who merited Christian veneration.

GLOSSARY

acanthus: A spiky, lustrous, deep green plant common to the Mediterranean basin; imitated in Corinthian capitals.
akroterion/a: Figures or ornaments at the apex or corners of a roof.
Amazonomachy: Legendary battle between Greeks and Amazons.
amphiprostyle: Columns only at the front and rear of a building.
anodos: The process of progressing upward.
anta: The enlarged "pilaster" end terminating the lateral walls in a Greek building.
architrave: the main beam and lowest member of an entablature.
ashlar: Masonry style with horizontal courses and vertical joints.
Attalid dynasty: Hellenistic kingdom (early third to late second century BC) whose capital was Pergamon.
basilica: A Christian church in the form of a long rectangular building, often with interior colonnades that form a nave and two side aisles.
Boethius: A Roman senator and philosopher whose most renowned work is the *Consolation of Philosophy,* written in the early 6th c. AD.
bothros: A hole or pit into which liquid offerings were poured.
bouleuterion: The building in which the council of citizens in a Greek city met.
cavea: The curved tiers of seats in a Greek theater.
caryatid: Female statue that takes the place of a column in supporting an entablature.
cella: The main room of a Greek temple, usually housing the statue of the deity to whom the temple is dedicated.
Centauromachy: Legendary battle between Greeks and centaurs.
chancel screen: A barrier of varying heights between the nave and the altar.
choragic: Relating to the chorus in Greek theatrical performances.
chthonic: Concerning, belonging to, or inhabiting subterranean Earth.
ciborium: A canopy in a sanctuary supported by freestanding columns.
clepsydra: An ancient water clock.
Clepsydra: A sacred spring on the slopes of the Athenian Acropolis.
coffer: a recessed panel in a dome, arch, flat ceiling, or cornice.
console: a curved bracket often used to support a cornice.
Corinthian capital: a column capital in the shape of a basket (kalathos) composed of acanthus leaves and volutes (scroll-like ornaments).

cornice: The upper member of an entablature; a projection from an exterior wall to carry rainwater away from the building or as ornamentation on an interior wall.
deal: Wood from coniferous trees, such as pine or fir.
crepidoma: The stepped platform on which a Greek temple or other structure stands.
diaconicon: The sacristy on the south side of a church, to the right of the altar, in which items necessary for rituals (e.g., vestments, books, etc.) were kept.
distyle-in-antis: Two columns standing between the antae.
Doric capital: A column capital consisting of a square element (abacus) on top of a semicircular element (echinus).
Doric frieze: The middle member of a Doric entablature comprising metopes and triglyphs.
entablature: The superstructure of a classical building that is supported by columns or a wall, commonly comprising an architrave, frieze course, ornamental moldings, and cornice.
Erechtheus: Mythical king and founder of the city-state of Athens.
exonarthex: The porch or entrance chamber leading to the narthex in a Byzantine church.
fascia(ae): A flat projecting band.
fillet: A narrow flat molding.
Gigantomachy: Mythic battle between the Olympian gods and the Giants, the children of Earth (Ge).
gnomon: The projecting rod-shaped element of a sundial that casts a shadow on the hour lines.
heroon: A commemorative monument for the worship of a demigod or heroized mortal (historical or mythological), often with funerary connotations.
Herulian: Pertaining to the Heruli, a Scandinavian or north-Germanic tribe that invaded Greece in the third century AD.
Hesiod: A Greek poet and contemporary of Homer. Hesiod is noted particularly for his *Theogony,* a genealogy of the gods, written ca. 700 BC.
Homer: A Greek poet, author of the *Iliad* and the *Odyssey,* written ca. 700 BC.
hexastyle: Having six columns across the façade.
iconostasis: A wall between the sanctuary and nave of a church that is adorned with icons or religious paintings.
imam: Man who leads prayers in a mosque.
imaret: a Turkish inn or hospice.
kalathos: Greek term for "basket"; in architecture, a reference to the bell-shaped core of the Corinthian capital surrounded by acanthus leaves and tendrils.
metope: A sunken panel (at times sculptured or painted with figures) between the triglyphs in a Doric frieze.
Metroön: The sanctuary of the Mother of the Gods.
Mevlevi dervishes: The sect of Whirling Dervishes founded by the Sufi poet Rumi in the thirteenth century.
mihrab: An apsidal niche in the wall of a mosque that indicates the direction of Mecca and where to face when praying.
minbar: The raised pulpit in a mosque from which an imam delivers his sermon.
naiskos: A small shrine or miniature temple, usually without a surrounding colonnade.
narthex: A vestibule spanning the width of a church that provides access to the nave.
nave: The main chamber of a church. It may be flanked by side aisles that are separated from the nave by columns.

Nike(ai): The goddess(es) of victory in Greek mythology.
opisthodomos: The porch at the rear of a Greek temple.
orrery: A mechanical model of the solar system.
ovolo: A convex molding with maximum projection near the top.
Panathenaia: An annual religious festival held in ancient Athens in honor of the goddess Athena.
Pandroseion: The open-air sanctuary dedicated to Pandrosos, daughter of the legendary first king of Athens, Cecrops; she was the first priestess of Athena.
parodos: One of the two lateral entrances (between the stage building and the *cavea* wall) leading into a Greek theater.
Pausanias: A Greek traveler and geographer who lived in the second century AD and is noted for his *Description of Greece,* in ten books (extant).
Pentelic marble: A fine white marble quarried from Mount Pentelikon, northeast of Athens, and used in the construction of the buildings on the Acropolis.
Pergamon: Ancient city in northwest Turkey and capital of the Attalid dynasty in the Hellenistic period.
peribolos: The walled enclosure of a sanctuary or *temenos* of a Greek deity.
peripteral: Surrounded by a peristyle.
peristyle: A surrounding colonnade.
pronaos: The porch at the front of a Greek temple.
Propylaea: The entrance gate building to the Athenian Acropolis (with five doorways).
propylon: A roofed gate building.
prostyle: Columns only across the front of a temple.
prothesis: A chamber on the north side of a church, to the left of the altar, where sacred vessels, bread, and wine were kept.
Ptolemaic dynasty: Founded by Ptolemy I, the Macedonian general and comrade of Alexander the Great, its kings and queens ruled Egypt in the Hellenistic period until the death of its last monarch, Cleopatra VII.
Seleucid dynasty: Founded by Seleukus I, the Macedonian general and comrade of Alexander the Great which ruled the eastern part of Alexander's empire in the Hellenistic period.
sima: Gutter on the roof of a building.
Slavs and Avars: Peoples living north of the Danube River in central and eastern Europe who invaded Greece in the late sixth century AD.
sphragis: In architecture, an identifying sign (e.g., a cross) indicating that a building is consecrated for Christian use.
stoa: A roofed portico supported by one or more rows of columns.
Sulla: Roman general active in the first century BC.
tegurium: A canopy supported by columns over an altar or a sarcophagus.
tekke: A building for meetings of members of the Sufi sect of Islam.
temenos: A sacred precinct, often surrounded by a wall.
templon: A barrier in a church separating the nave from the altar.
tetraconch: An architectural form, usually of a religious building, with four apses of equal size, one in each direction.
tetrastyle: Having a four-columned façade.
triglyph: Carved panels in a Doric frieze with vertical divisions, alternating with metopes.

GLOSSARY

Triton: In Greek mythology, the son of Poseidon; a merman, usually portrayed with the lower body of a marine animal.
Valerian: Roman emperor who reigned AD 253–260.
Varro: Roman scholar and author of the first century BC.
Visigoths: A Germanic tribe that invaded Greece in the late sixth century.
Vitruvius: Roman architect and military engineer of the first century BC.

BIBLIOGRAPHY

Alcock, S. E. 2002. *Archaeologies of the Greek Past. Landscapes, Monuments, and Memories.* Cambridge.

Antikythera Mechanism Research Project. n.d. http://www.antikythera-mechanism.gr/.

Armstrong, J. E., and J. M. Camp. 1977. "Notes on a Water Clock in the Athenian Agora." *Hesperia* 46: 147–61.

Atasoy, N. 1992. "Dervish Dress and Ritual: The Mevlevi Tradition." In *The Dervish Lodge: Architecture, Art, and Sufism in Ottoman Turkey,* ed. R. Lifchez, 253–68. Berkeley.

Babinger, F. C. H. 1978. *Mehmed the Conqueror and His Time.* Princeton.

Baldassari, P. 1998. *ΣΕΒΑΣΤΩΙ ΣΩΤΗΡΙ: Edilizia monumentale ad Atene durante il saeculum Augustum.* Rome.

Barringer, J. 2009. "A New Approach to the Temple of Hephaestus: Heroic Models in the Athenian Agora." In *Structure, Image, Ornament: Architectural Sculpture in the Greek World,* eds. P. Schultz and R. von den Hoff, 105–20. Proceedings of an International Conference Held at the American School of Classical Studies, November 27–28, 2004. Oxford.

Bitton-Ashkelony, B. 2005. *Encountering the Sacred: The Debate on Christian Pilgrimage in Late Antiquity.* Berkeley.

Bodnar, E. W. 1960. *Cyriacus of Ancona and Athens. Collection Latomus* 43, Brussels-Berchem.

Bodnar, E. W. 1970a. "Athens in April 1436: Part I," *Archaeology* 23: 96–105.

Bodnar, E. W. 1970b. "Athens in April 1436: Part II," *Archaeology* 23: 188–199.

Bohtz, C. H. 1981. *Das Demeter-Heiligtum. Altertümer von Pergamon,* Vol. 13. Berlin.

Bouras, C. 2010. "Το κτισμένο περιβάλλον και τα μνημεία." In *Βυζαντινή Αθήνα: 10ος-12ος αι,* Athens.

Braun, J. 1924. *Der christliche Altar in seiner geschichtlichen Entwicklung.* Munich.

Brown, P. 1981. *The Cult of the Saints: Its Rise and Function in Latin Christianity.* Chicago.

Callaghan, P. J. 1981. "On the Date of the Great Altar of Pergamon," *BICS* 28,115–21.

Cam, M.-T. 2001. *M. Cetius Faventinus: Abrégé d'architecture privée.* Paris.

Camp, J. M. 2001. *Archaeology of Athens.* New Haven.

———. 2010. *The Athenian Agora Site Guide.* Princeton.

Carey, J., ed. 2003. *Eyewitness to History.* New York.

Castrén, P. 1994. "General Aspects of Life in Post-Herulian Athens." In *Post-Herulian Athens. Aspects of Life and Culture,* ed. P. Castrén, 1–14. Helsinki.

———. 1999. "Paganism and Christianity in Athens and Vicinity during the Fourth to Sixth Centuries A.D.." In *The Idea and Ideal of the Town between Late Antiquity and the Early Middle Ages,* eds. G. P. Brogiolo and B. Ward-Perkins, 211–23. Leiden.

Chandler, R. 1776. *Travels in Greece.* Oxford.

Chaniotis, A., and J. Mylonopoulos. 2004. "Epigraphic Bulletin for Greek Religion 2001." *Kernos* 17: 187–249.

Chatzidakis, M. 1960. *Byzantine Athens.* Athens.

Clarke, E. D. 1818. *Travels in Various Countries of Europe, Asia and Africa,* Part 2. London.

Connelly, J. B. 2014. *The Parthenon Enigma. A new understanding of the West's most iconic building and the people who made it.* New York.

Coppola, D. 2010. *Anemoi: Morfologia dei Venti nell'Immaginario della Grecia Arcaica.* Napoli.

Cornelison, S. J. 2004. "Art Imitates Architecture: The Saint Philip Reliquary in Renaissance Florence." *ArtBull* 86: 642–58.

Corso, A. 1997. "Vitruvius and Attic Monuments." *BSA* 92: 373–400.

———. 2009. "A Few Thoughts on the Tower of the Winds." In *Κερμάτια φιλίας: Studies in Honour of Ioannis Touratsoglou,* Vol. 2, ed. S. Drougou et al., 314–19. Athens.

Couchaud, A. 1842. *Choix d'églises byzantines en Grèce.* Paris.

Coulton, J. J. 1976. *The Architectural Development of the Greek Stoa.* Oxford.

Culley, G. R. 1975. "The Restoration of Sanctuaries in Attica: *IG* II^2, 1035." *Hesperia* 44: 207–23.

———. 1977. "The Restoration of Sanctuaries in Attica, II." *Hesperia* 46: 282–98.

Cutler, A. 1993–1994. "The Christian Wall Paintings in the Parthenon: Interpreting a Lost Monument." *Deltion XAE* 17: 171–80.

Dalton, J. 1752. *Remarks on XII Historical Designs of Raphael, and the Musaeum Graecum et Aegyptiacum, or, Antiquities of Greece and Egypt:* 20–21. London.

Dalton, R. 1791. *Antiquities and Views in Greece and Egypt with the Manners and Customs of the Inhabitants from Drawings Made on the Spot, A.D. 1749.* London.

Damianidis, K. 2011. "Roman Ship Graffiti in the Tower of the Winds in Athens." *ArchKorrBl* 41: 85–99.

D'Andria, F. 2001. "Hierapolis of Phrygia: Its Evolution in Hellenistic and Roman Times." In *Urbanism in Western Asia Minor,* ed. D. Parrish, 94–115. Portsmouth, RI.

Dankoff, R. 1989. "The Languages of the World According to Evliya Çelebi." *J. Turkish Studies* 13: 23–32.

Dankoff, R., F. Faroqhi, and G. Hagen. 2004. *An Ottoman Mentality: The World of Evliya Çelebi.* Leiden and Boston.

Dankoff, R., and S. Kim. 2010. *An Ottoman Traveller: Selections from the 'Book of Travels' of Evliya Çelebi.* London.

Davesne, A. 1982. *La Frise du Temple d'Artémis à Magnésie du Méandre: Catalogue des Fragments du Musée du Louvre.* Paris.

Day, J. 1942. *An Economic History of Athens under Roman Domination.* New York.

Delehaye, H. 1933. *Les Origines du Culte des Martyrs.* Brussels.

De Luca, G. and W. Radt. 1999. *Sondagen im Fundament des Grossen Altars.* Pergamenische Forschungen 12. Berlin.

Dickie, J. 1978. "Allah and Eternity: Mosques, Madrasas, and Tombs." In *Architecture of the Islamic World,* ed. G. Michell, 15–47. New York.

Dinsmoor, W. B. 1934. "The Repair of the Athena Parthenos: A Story of Five Dowels." *AJA* 38: 93–106.
———. 1941. "Observations on the Temple of Hephaestus." *Hesperia,* Suppl. 5: 1–171.
———. 1975. *The Architecture of Ancient Greece.* New York. (Reprint of the 1950 3rd edition.)
Dodwell, E. 1819. *A Classical and Topographical Tour through Greece during the Years 1801, 1805, and 1806,* Vol. 1. London.
D'Ooge, M. L. 1908. *The Acropolis of Athens.* London.
Durm, J. 1910. *Handbuch der Architektur,* Vol. II. Pt. 1, *Die Baukunst der Griechen.* Leipzig.
Eibner C. 2013. "Astronomisches aus Salzburg und Heron von Alexandria." In *Calamus: Festschrift für Herbert Graßl zum 65: Geburtstag,* eds. Monika Frass, Rupert Breitwieser, and Georg Nightingale, 177–83. Wiesbaden (Philippika, 57).
Etienne, R., and J.-P. Braun. 1986. *Ténos I: Le Sanctuaire de Poseidon et d'Amphitrite.* Athens.
Evans, J. 1999. "The Material Culture of Greek Astronomy." *JHA* 30: 237–307.
Ferguson, E. 2009. *Baptism in the Early Church: History, Theology, and Liturgy in the First Five Centuries.* Grand Rapids, MI.
Frank, G. 2000a. *The Memory of the Eyes: Pilgrims to Living Saints in Christian Late Antiquity.* Berkeley.
———. 2000b. "The Pilgrim's Gaze in the Age before Icons." In *Visuality before and beyond the Renaissance,* ed. R. S. Nelson, 98–115. Cambridge.
Frantz, A. 1965. "From Paganism to Christianity in the Temples of Athens." *DOP* 19: 187–205.
Frantz, A., H. A. Thompson, and J. Travlos. 1969. "The 'Temple of Apollo Pythios' on Sikinos." *AJA* 73: 397–422.
———. 1988. *Late Antiquity: A.D. 267–700. The Athenian Agora,* Vol. 24. Princeton.
Freeth, T., and A. R. Jones. 2012. "The Cosmos in the Antikythera Mechanism." *ISAW Papers* 4.
Friedlander, S. 1992. *The Whirling Dervishes: Being an Account of the Sufi Order Known as the Mevlevis, and Its Founder, the Poet and Mystic Mevlana Jalalu'ddin Rumi.* Albany.
Geary, P. 1986. "Sacred Commodities: The Circulation of Medieval Relics." In *The Social Life of Things: Commodities in Cultural Perspective,* ed. A. Appadurai, 169–91. Cambridge.
———. 1990. *Furta Sacra: Thefts of Relics in the Central Middle Ages.* Princeton.
Gibbs, S. L. 1976. *Greek and Roman Sundials.* New Haven.
Goette, H. R. 2001. *Athens, Attica and the Megarid: An Archaeological Guide.* London and New York.
Goodwin, G. 1992. "Dervish Architecture of Anatolia." In *The Dervish Lodge: Architecture, Art, and Sufism in Ottoman Turkey,* ed. R. Lifchez, 57–69. Berkeley.
Grabar, A. 1946. *Martyrium: Recherches sur le Culte des Reliques et l'Art Chrétien Antique.* Paris.
Granger, F. 1983. Vitruvius. *De Architectura.* Loeb Classical Library. Cambridge, MA.
Greco, E. 2014. *Topografia di Atene. Sviluppo urbano e monumenti dalle origini al III secolo d.C.,* Vol. 3, Part 1. Athens/Paestum.
Gregory, T. E. 1986. "The Survival of Paganism in Christian Greece: A Critical Essay." *AJP* 107: 229–42.
Grig, L. 2004. *Making Martyrs in Late Antiquity.* London.
Habicht, C. 1990. "Athens and the Attalids in the Second Century B.C." *Hesperia* 59: 561–77.
———. 1996. "Salamis in der Zeit nach Sulla." *ZPE* 111: 85.
Hamiaux, M. 2007. *La Victoire de Samothrace.* Paris.

Hamiaux, M., L. Laugler, and J.-L. Martinex, eds. 2014. *La Victoire de Samothrace: Redécouvrir un chef-d'oeuvre.* Paris.
Hampe, R. 1967. *Kult der Winde in Athen und Kreta.* Heidelberg.
Hansen, E. V. 1971. *The Attalids of Pergamon.* Ithaca and London.
Hansen, M. H. 1999. *The Athenian Democracy in the Age of Demosthenes: Structure, Principles and Ideology.* Translated by J. A. Crook. Norman OK.
Hanson, R. P. C. 1978. "The Transformation of Pagan Temples into Churches in the Early Christian Centuries." *J. Semitic Studies* 23: 257–67.
Haselberger, L. 2014. *The Horologium of Augustus: Debate and Context.* Portsmouth, RI.
Hesberg, H. von. 1980. *Konsolengeisa des Hellenismus und der frühen Kaiserzeit.* Mainz.
Hoepfner, W. 1993. "Zum Mausoleum von Belevi." *AA* 108: 111–23, fig. 10.
Hoff, M. C. 1994. "The So-Called Agoranomion and the Imperial Cult in Julio-Claudian Athens." *AA* 109: 93–117.
———. 1997. "*Laceratae Athenae:* Sulla's Siege of Athens in 87/86 B.C. and Its Aftermath." In *The Romanization of Athens,* eds. M.C. Hoff and S. I Rotroff, 33–51. Oxford.
Holum, K. G., and G. Vikan. 1979. "The Trier Ivory, *Adventus* Ceremonial, and the Relics of St. Stephen." *DOP* 33: 113–33.
Hooper, W. D., and H. B. Ash. 1993. Varro. *De Re Rustica.* Loeb Classical Library. Cambridge MA.
Horowitz, W. 1998. *Mesopotamian Cosmic Geography.* Winona Lake, IN.
Hurwit, J. M. 1999. *The Athenian Acropolis: History, Mythology, and Archaeology from the Neolithic Era to the Present.* Cambridge.
———. 2004. *The Acropolis in the Age of Pericles.* Cambridge.
Iliades, Y. 2006. "The Orientation of Byzantine Churches in Eastern Macedonia and Thrace." *MAA* 6: 209–14.
Inwood, H. W. 1827. *The Erechtheum at Athens.* London.
James, M. R. 1955. The Apocryphal New Testament. Oxford.
Jensen, R. M. 2011. *Living Water: Images, Symbols, and Settings of Early Christian Baptism.* Leiden.
Johnston, P. F. 1985. *Ship and Boat Models in Ancient Greece.* Annapolis, MD.
Kaldellis, A. 2009. *The Christian Parthenon: Classicism and Pilgrimage in Byzantine Athens.* Cambridge.
Karanastasi, P. 2014. "Die Reliefdarstellung der Winde." In H. J. Kienast, *Der Turm der Winde in Athen.* Wiesbaden.
Karivieri, A. 1994. "The So-Called Library of Hadrian and the Tetraconch Church." In *Post-Herulian Athens. Aspects of Life and Culture,* ed. P. Castrén, 89–113. Helsinki.
Karoglou, K. 2016. "Trends in Hellenistic Sculpture." In *Pergamon and the Hellenistic Kingdoms of the Ancient World,* eds. C. A. Picón and S. Hemingway, 62–69. New Haven.
Kästner, V. 2016. "Pergamon and the Attalids." In *Pergamon and the Hellenistic Kingdom of the Ancient World,* eds. C. A. Picón and S. Hemingway, 32–39. New Haven.
Kazanaki-Lappa, M. 2002. "Medieval Athens." In *The Economic History of Byzantium: From the Seventh through the Fifteenth Century,* ed. A. E. Laiou. *DOS* 39: 639–46. Washington, DC.
Keyes, C. W. 1928. Cicero. *On the Republic.* Loeb Classical Library. Cambridge, MA.
Kienast, H. J. 1993. "Untersuchungen am Turm der Winde." *AA:* 271–75.
———. 1997. "The Tower of the Winds in Athens: Hellenistic or Roman?" In *The Romanization of Athens,* eds. Michael C. Hoff and Susan I. Rotroff, 53–65. Oxford.

———. 2014. *Der Turm der Winde in Athen.* Wiesbaden.

Kiilerich, B. 2005. "Making Sense of the Spolia in the Little Metropolis in Athens." *ArtMed* 4.2: 95–114.

———. 2013. "From Temple to Church: The Redefinition of the Sacred Landscape on the Acropolis." In *Sacred Sites and Holy Places: Exploring the Sacralization of Landscape through Time and Space,* eds. S. W. Nordeide and S. Brink, 187–214. Turnhout, Belgium.

King, D. A. 1982. "Astronomical Alignments in Medieval Islamic Religious Architecture." *AnnNYAcadSci* 385: 303–12.

Kirsch, J. P. 1911. "Philip, Saint, Apostle." *CathEnc,* Vol. 11, 799. New York.

Knackfuss, H. 1908. *Das Rathaus von Milet. Milet* Vol. 1.2. Berlin.

———. 1924. *Der Südmarkt und die benachbarten Bauanlagen. Milet* Vol. 1.7. Berlin.

Koch, G. 1996. *Early Christian Art and Architecture.* London.

Korres, M. 1994. "The History of the Acropolis Monuments." In *Acropolis Restoration: The CCAM Interventions,* ed. R. Economakis, 43–51. London.

———. 1996. "The Parthenon from Antiquity to the 19th Century." In *The Parthenon and Its Impact in Modern Times,* ed. P. Tournikiotis, 137–61. Athens.

Korres, M., et al. 2003. *Athens from the Classical Period to the Present Day (5th Century B.C.–A.D. 2000).* New Castle, DE.

Koukouli-Chrysanthaki, Ch., and Ch. Bakirtzis. 1995. *Philippi.* Athens.

Kreiser, K. 1992. "The Dervish Living." In *The Dervish Lodge: Architecture, Art, and Sufism in Ottoman Turkey,* ed. R. Lifchez, 49–56. Berkeley.

Kritoboulos, M. 1954. *History of Mehmed the Conqueror.* Translated by C. T. Riggs. Princeton.

Lapidus, I. M. 1992. "Sufism and Ottoman Islamic Society." In *The Dervish Lodge: Architecture, Art, and Sufism in Ottoman Turkey,* ed. R. Lifchez, 15–32. Berkeley.

Laqueur, H.-P. 1992. "Dervish Gravestones." In *The Dervish Lodge: Architecture, Art, and Sufism in Ottoman Turkey,* ed. R. Lifchez, 284–94. Berkeley.

La Riche, W. 1996. *Alexandria: The Sunken City.* London.

Lauter, H. 1979. "Bemerkungen zur späthellenistischen Baukunst in Mittelitalien." *JdI* 94: 390–459.

———. 1988. "Hellenistische Sepulkralarchitektur auf Rhodos, mit einem Anhang: Rhodisch-Koische Nikealtäre und die Bildhauerswerkstatt des Turmes der Winde zu Athen." In *Archaeology in the Dodecanese,* eds. S. Dietz and I. Papachristodoulou, 155–63. Copenhagen.

Lawrence, A. W. 1996. *Greek Architecture.* New Haven and London.

Lefantzis, M. and J. Tae Jensen. 2009. "The Athenian Asklepieion on the South Slope of the Akropolis: Early Development, ca. 420–360 B.C.," in: *Aarhus Studies in Mediterranean Antiquity: Aspects of Ancient Greek Cult: Context - Ritual - Iconography* (1), eds. P. Schultz, B. Wickkiser, and G. Hinge, 91–124. Aarhus.

Lehmann, K., et al. 1998. *Samothrace: A Guide to the Excavations and the Museum.* Thessaloniki.

Lehmann, P. W. 1969. *The Hieron.* Samothrace Vol. 3. Princeton.

Levi, P. 1984. Pausanias. *Guide to Greece.* Middlesex, Eng.

Lifchez, R. 1992. "The Lodges of Istanbul." In *The Dervish Lodge: Architecture, Art, and Sufism in Ottoman Turkey,* ed. R. Lifchez, 73–129. Berkeley.

Limberis, V. 1994. *Divine Heiress: The Virgin Mary and the Creation of Christian Constantinople.* London and New York.

———. 2005. "Ecclesiastical Ambiguities: Corinth in the Fourth and Fifth Centuries." In *Urban Religion in Roman Corinth: Interdisciplinary Approaches,* eds. D. Showalter and S. Friesen, 443–57. Cambridge, MA.

———. 2011. *Architects of Piety: The Cappadocian Fathers and the Cult of the Martyrs.* Oxford.

MacKay, P. A. 1968. "Acrocorinth in 1668: A Turkish Account." *Hesperia* 37: 386–97.

———. 1969. "A Turkish Description of the Tower of the Winds." *AJA* 73: 468–69.

Mango, C. 1990. "Constantine's Mausoleum and the Translation of Relics." *ByzZeit* 83: 51–62.

———. 1995. "Conversion of the Parthenon into a Church." *Deltion XAE* 18: 201–03.

Maraval, P. 2002. "The Earliest Phase of Christian Pilgrimage in the Near East." *DOP* 56: 63–74.

Matthews, C. R. 2002. *Philip, Apostle and Evangelist: Configurations of a Tradition.* Boston.

McCredie, J. R. 1992. *The Rotunda of Arsinoe.* Samothrace Vol. 7. Princeton.

McGuckin, J. A. 2001. *St. Gregory of Nazianzus: An Intellectual Biography.* Crestwood, NY.

Meer, F. van der. 1961. *Augustine the Bishop: The Life and Work of a Father of the Church.* London and New York.

Miles, M. M. 1980. "The Date of the Temple on the Ilissus River." *Hesperia* 49: 309–25.

———. 2008. *Art as Plunder: The Ancient Origins of Debate about Cultural Property.* Cambridge.

Miller, S. G. 1995. "Architecture as Evidence for the Identity of the Early Polis." In *Sources for the Ancient Greek City-State,* ed. M. H. Hansen, 201–44. Copenhagen.

Miller, W. 1908. *The Latins in the Levant: A History of Frankish Greece (1204–1566).* New York.

Mommsen, A. 1868. *Athenae Christianae.* Leipzig.

Morgan, C., et al. 2009–2010. "Corinthia." In *AR* 56: 21–41.

Morgan, M. H. 1914. Vitruvius. *The Ten Books on Architecture.* Cambridge, MA.

Morrow, K. D. 1985. *Greek Footwear and the Dating of Sculpture.* Madison.

Noble, J. V., and D. J. de Solla Price. 1968. "The Water Clock in the Tower of the Winds." *AJA* 72: 345–55, pls. 112–18.

Obrist, B. 1997. "Wind Diagrams and Medieval Cosmology." *Speculum* 72: 33–84.

Oliver, J. H. 1941. "The Sacred Gerusia." *Hesperia,* Suppl. 6.

———. 1972. "On the Hellenic policy of Augustus and Agrippa in 27 B.C." *AJP* 93: 190–97.

Omont, H. 1898. *Athènes au XVIIe Siècle.* Paris.

Orlandos, A. K. 1919. "Εργα αναστηλώσεως." *ArchDelt,* Annex A: 14–16.

———. 1936. Ἀρχεῖον των βυζαντινών μνημείων της Ελλάδος, II, 207–16. Athens.

———. 1964. "Εκθεσις περί των ανασκαφών Βιβλιοθήκης Αδριανού και Ρωμαικής Αγοράς." *ArchEph:* 6–59, esp. 59, fig. 112.

Ousterhout, R. 2005. "'Bestride the Very Peak of Heaven': The Parthenon after Antiquity." In *The Parthenon from Antiquity to the Present,* ed. J. Neils, 293–329. Cambridge.

Pallis A. 1951. *In the Days of the Janissaries: Old Turkish Life as Depicted in the 'Travel-Book' of Evliya Chelebi.* London and New York.

Papini, M. 2016. "Commemorations of Victory: Attalid Monuments to the Defeat of the Galatians." In *Pergamon and the Hellenistic Kingdoms of the Ancient World,* ed. C. A. Picón and S. Hemingway, 40–43. New Haven.

Parsons, A. W. 1943. "Klepsydra and the Paved Court of Pythion." *Hesperia* 12: 191–267.

Paton, J. M., ed. 1927. *The Erechtheum.* Cambridge.

———. 1951. *Chapters on Medieval and Renaissance Visitors to Greek Lands.* Princeton.
Pittakiés, K. S. 1835. *L'ancienne Athènes, ou La description des antiquités d'Athènes et de ses environs.* Athens.
Plommer, H. 1973. *Vitruvius and Later Roman Building Manuals.* Cambridge.
Pococke, R. 1745. *A Description of the East and Some Other Countries* II.2. London.
Preger, T. 1975. *Scriptores Originum Constantinopolitanarum.* New York.
Price, D. J. de Solla. 1964. "Automata and the Origins of Mechanism and Mechanistic Philosophy." *TechnolCult* 5: 9–23.
———. 1967. "Piecing Together an Ancient Puzzle: The Tower of the Winds." *Natl Geog* Vol. 131.4: 586–96.
———. 1976. *Science since Babylon.* New Haven.
Rackham, H. 1942. Pliny the Elder. Natural History. Loeb Classical Library. Cambridge, MA.
Ridgway, B. S. 1981. *Fifth Century Styles in Greek Sculpture.* Princeton.
———. 1990. Hellenistic Sculpture I: The Styles of ca. 331–200 B.C. Madison.
———. 2000. *Hellenistic Sculpture II: The Styles of ca. 200–100 B.C.* Madison.
———. 2002. *Hellenistic Sculpture III: The Styles of ca. 100–31 B.C.* Madison.
Robertson, N. 1996. "Athena's Shrines and Festivals." In *Worshipping Athena: Panathenaia and Parthenon,* ed. J. Neils, 27–77. Madison.
Robinson, H. S. 1943. "The Tower of the Winds and the Roman Market-Place." *AJA* 47: 291–305.
———. 1984. "Review of von Freeden." *AJA* 88: 423–25.
Rose, H. J. 1959. *A Handbook of Greek Mythology,* 64–65. New York.
Rottländer, R. C. A., W. Heinz, and W. Neumaier. 1989. "Untersuchungen am Turm der Winde in Athen." *Öjh* 59: 55–92.
Saradi-Mendelovici, H. 1990. *Christian Attitudes toward Pagan Monuments in Late Antiquity. DOP* 44: 47–61.
Sayer, R. 1759. *Ruins of Athens, with Remains and Other Valuable Antiquities in Greece.* London.
Schaefer, B. 2005. "Discovery of the Lost Star Catalog of Hipparchus on the Farnese Atlas." Abstract from a talk presented to the American Astronomical Society, San Diego, CA.
Schaldach, K. 2014. "Zu den Sonnenuhren des Andronikos." In H. J. Kienast, *Der Turm der Winde in Athen,* 197–226. Wiesbaden.
Schazmann, P. 1923. *Das Gymnasion: Der Tempelbezirk der Hera Basileia. AvP* VI. Berlin and Leipzig.
Schmalz, G. C. R. 2008. "Inscribing a Ritualized Past: The Attic Restoration Decree *IG* II[2] 1035 and Cultural Memory in Augustan Athens." *Eulimene* 9: 11–46.
———. 2009. *Augustan and Julio-Claudian Athens: A New Epigraphy and Prosopography.* Boston.
SEG, 1981, vol. 31, no. 107: "Athens. Decree on the restoration of sanctuaries, date?"; H. W. Pleket and R. S. Stroud, eds.
SEG, 198, vol. 33, no. 136: "Athens. Decree on the restoration of sanctuaries, date?"; H. W. Pleket and R. S. Stroud, eds.
Setton, K. M. 1944. "Athens in the Late Twelfth Century." *Speculum* 19: 179–208.
———. 1975. *Athens in the Middle Ages.* London.
———. 1991. *Venice, Austria, and the Turks in the Seventeenth Century.* Philadelphia.

Seznec, J. 1953. *The Survival of the Pagan Gods: The Mythological Tradition and Its Place in Renaissance Humanism and Art.* New York.

Shear, T. L. 1981. "Athens: From City-state to Provincial Town." *Hesperia* 50: 356–77.

Simon, E. 1997. *LIMC* 8, *s.v.* "Venti". Düsseldorf.

Sironen, E. 1994. "Life and Administration of Late Roman Attica in the Light of Public Inscriptions." In *Post-Herulian Athens. Aspects of Life and Culture,* ed. P. Castrén, 15–62. Helsinki.

Slavitt, D. R. 2008. Boethius, *Consolation of Philosophy.* Cambridge, MA.

Small, D. B. 1980. "A Proposal for the Reuse of the Tower of the Winds." *AJA* 84: 96–99.

Smith, D. M. 2015. "Newsround." *AR* 61: 12–33.

Smith, R. R. R. 1985. "Review of Von Freeden." *JHS* 105: 230–31.

Soteriou, G. A. 1927. "Agios Philippos." In *Eureterion ton Mesaionikon Mnemeion tes Ellados,* Part A. Athens.

Spieser, J-M. 2001. "Ambrose's Foundations at Milan and the Question of Martyria." In *Urban and Religious Spaces in Late Antiquity and Early Byzantium,* ed. J.-M. Spieser, ch. 6, 1–13. Aldershot, Hampshire.

Stewart, A. 1990. *Greek Sculpture: An Exploration.* New Haven.

———. 2004. *Attalos, Athens, and the Acropolis: The Pergamene 'Little Barbarians' and Their Roman and Renaissance Legacy.* Cambridge.

———. 2016. "The Nike of Samothrace: Another View." *AJA:* 399–410.

Stuart, J., and N. Revett. 1762. *The Antiquities of Athens,* Vol. 1. London.

———. 1825. *The Antiquities of Athens,* Vol. 1. London.

Sweetman, R. J. 2015. "Memory, Tradition, and Christianization of the Peloponnese." *AJA* 119: 501–31.

Tanman, M. B. 1992. "Settings for the Veneration of Saints." In *The Dervish Lodge: Architecture, Art, and Sufism in Ottoman Turkey,* ed. R. Lifchez, 130–71. Berkeley.

Tanoulas, T. 1994. "The Propylaea and the Western Access of the Acropolis." In *Acropolis Restoration: The CCAM Interventions,* ed. R. Economakis, 52–67. London.

Thiersch, H. 1909. *Pharos, Antike, Islam und Occident: Ein Beitrag zur Architekturgeschichte.* Leipzig and Berlin.

Thompson, H. A. 1954. "Excavations in the Athenian Agora." *Hesperia* 33: 37–38.

———. 1959. "Athenian Twilight: A.D. 267–600." *JRS* 49: 61–72.

———. 1987. "The Impact of Roman Architects and Architecture on Athens: 170 B.C.–A.D. 170." In *Roman Architecture in the Greek World,* ed. S. Macready and F. H. Thompson, 1–17. London.

Thompson, H. A., and R. E. Wycherley. 1972. *The Agora of Athens: The History, Shape and Uses of an Ancient City. Athenian Agora* Vol. 14. Princeton.

Thür, H. 1990. "Arsinoë IV, eine Schwester Kleopatras VII, Grabinhaberin des Oktogons von Ephesus? Ein Vorschlag." *JÖAI* 60: 43–56.

Travlos, J. 1971. *Pictorial Dictionary of Ancient Athens.* London.

———. 1973. "Η πυρπόλησις του Παρθενώνος υπό των Ερούλων και η επισκευή του κατά τους χρόνους του αυτοκράτορος Ιουλιανού." *ArchEph:* 218–36.

Travlos J., and A. Frantz. 1965. "St. Dionysios." *Hesperia* 34: 157–202.

Tsafrir, Y. 1993. "The Development of Ecclesiastical Architecture in Palestine." In *Ancient Churches Revealed,* ed. Yoram Tsafrir, 1–16. Jerusalem.

Underwood, P. A. 1950. "The Fountain of Life in Manuscripts of the Gospels." *DOP* 5: 43–138.

Verhoef, E. 2008. "Syncretism in the Church of Philippi." *HTS* 64: 697–714.

Verzone, P. 1978. "Le ultime fasi vitali di Hierapolis di Frigia." In *Proc. Xth Intl. Cong. Class. Archaeology*, 849–55. Ankara.

Vlachou, M. 2010. "Le Monument des Taureaux: Une consecration d'Antigone le Borgne et de Demetrios Poliorcète?" *Mare Internum Archeologia e Culture del Mediterraneo, Vol. 2*: 71–80.

Volanakis, J. 1976. *Τα παλαιοχριστιανικά βαρτιστήρια της Ελλάδος*. Athens.

von Freeden, J. 1983. *Oikia Kyrrestou: Studien zum sogenannten Turm der Winde in Athen*. Rome.

Wachsmuth, C. 1874. *Die Stadt Athen im Alterthum*, Vol. 1. Leipzig.

Ward-Perkins, B. 1999. "Re-using the Architectural Legacy of the Past, *entre idéologie et pragmatisme*." In *The Idea and Ideal of the Town between Late Antiquity and the Early Middle Ages*, ed. G. P. Brogiolo and B. Ward-Perkins, 225–44. Leiden.

Webb, P. A. 1996. *Hellenistic Architectural Sculpture*. Madison.

———. 1998. "The Functions of the Sanctuary of Athena and the Pergamon Altar (the Heroon of Telephos) in the Attalid Building Program." In *Stephanos: Studies in Honor of Brunilde Sismondo Ridgway*, eds. K. J. Hartswick and M. C. Sturgeon, 241–54. Philadelphia.

———. 2015. Review of H. J. Kienast, *Der Turm der Winde in Athen*, Wiesbaden (2014) in: *Bryn Mawr Classical Review* 2015.09.15.

Welter, G. 1938. "Das choregische Denkmal des Thrasyllos." *AA*: 34–67.

Wescoat, B. D. 2005. "Buildings for Votive Ships on Delos and Samothrace." In *Architecture and Archaeology in the Cyclades: Papers in Honour of J. J. Coulton*, ed. M. Yeloulanou and M. Samatopoulou, 153–72. Oxford.

Wheler, G., and J. Spon. 1682. *A Journey into Greece by George Wheler, Esq., in the Company of Dr. Spon of Lyons: In Six Books . . . with Variety of Sculptures*. London.

Winnefeld, H. 1910. *Die Friese des grossen Altars*. *AvP* III.2. Berlin.

Wortley, J. 2009a. "The Byzantine Component of the Relic-Hoard of Constantinople." In *Studies on the Cult of Relics in Byzantium up to 1204*. Ch. 2, 353–78. Farnham, Eng.

———. 2009b. "The Legend of Constantine the Relic-Provider." In *Studies on the Cult of Relics in Byzantium up to 1204*. Ch. 3, 487–96. Farnham, Eng.

———. 2009c. "The Earliest Relic-Importation to Constantinople." In *Studies on the Cult of Relics in Byzantium up to 1204*. Ch. 4, 207–25. Farnham, Eng.

Wycherley, R. E. 1978. *The Stones of Athens*. Princeton.

Yasin, A. M. 2009. *Saints and Church Spaces in the Late Antique Mediterranean: Architecture, Cult, and Community*. Cambridge.

Yaylali, A. 1976. *Der Fries des Artemisions von Magnesia am Mäander*. *IstMitt* BH 15.

Yürekli, Z. 2012. *Architecture and Hagiography in the Ottoman Empire: The Politics of Bektashi Shrines in the Classical Age*. Farnham, Surrey, Eng.

Zarinebaf, F. 2005. "Soldiers into Tax-Farmers and Reaya into Sharecroppers: The Ottoman Morea in the Early Modern Period." In *A Historical and Economic Geography of Ottoman Greece: The Southwestern Morea in the Eighteenth Century*. *Hesperia* Suppl. 34: 9–47.

Zarinebaf, F., J. L. Davis, and J. Bennet. 2005. "Conclusions." In *A Historical and Economic Geography of Ottoman Greece: The Southwestern Morea in the Eighteenth Century*. *Hesperia*, Suppl. 34: 211–14.

Ziebarth, E. 1899. "Ein griechischer Reisebericht des fünfzehnten Jahrhunderts." *AM* 24, 72–88.

ILLUSTRATIONS

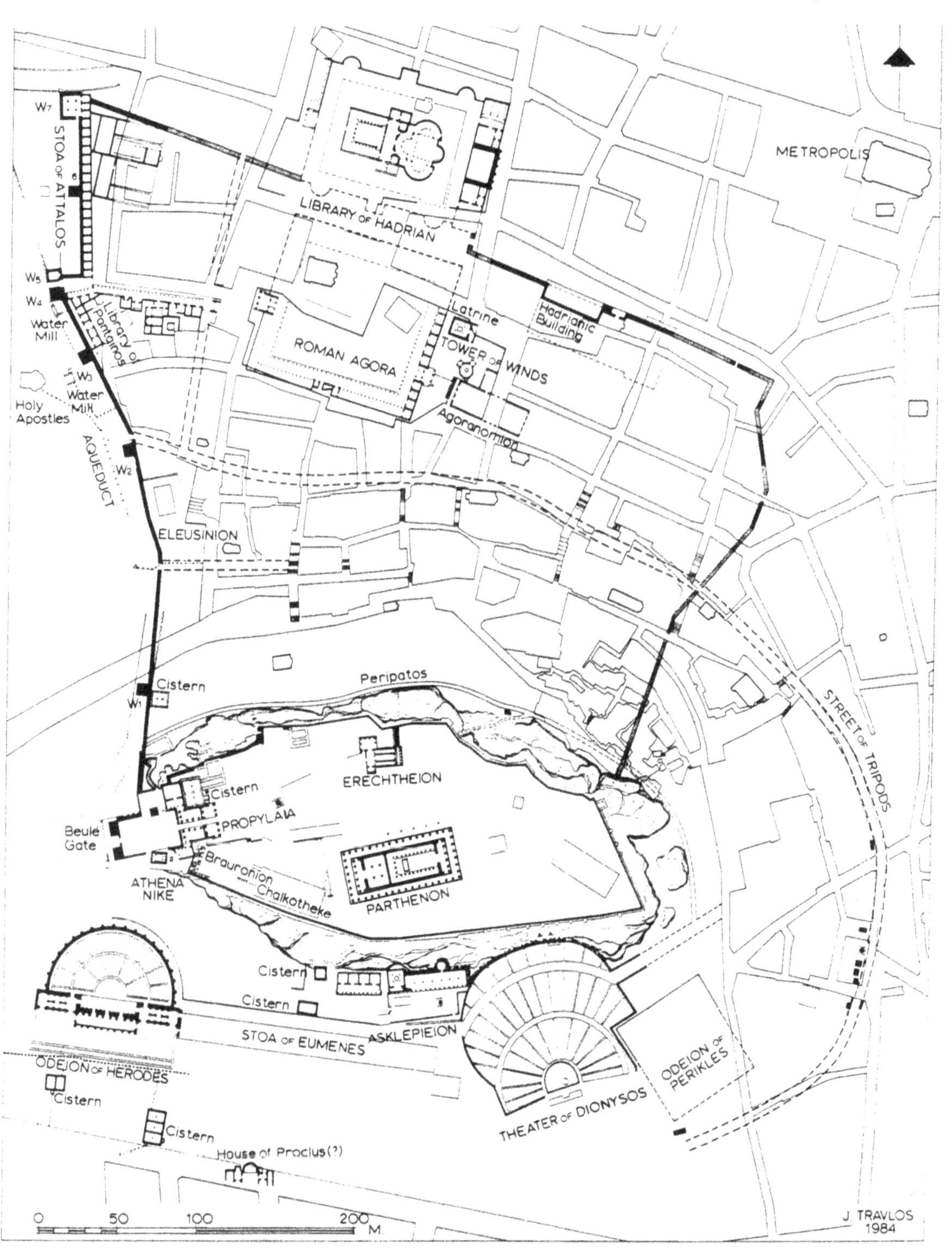

1. Map of central Athens within the Post-Herulian Wall (fifth century AD).

2. View of the Tower from the north.

3. Reconstruction of the exterior of the Tower by Stuart and Revett (1762).

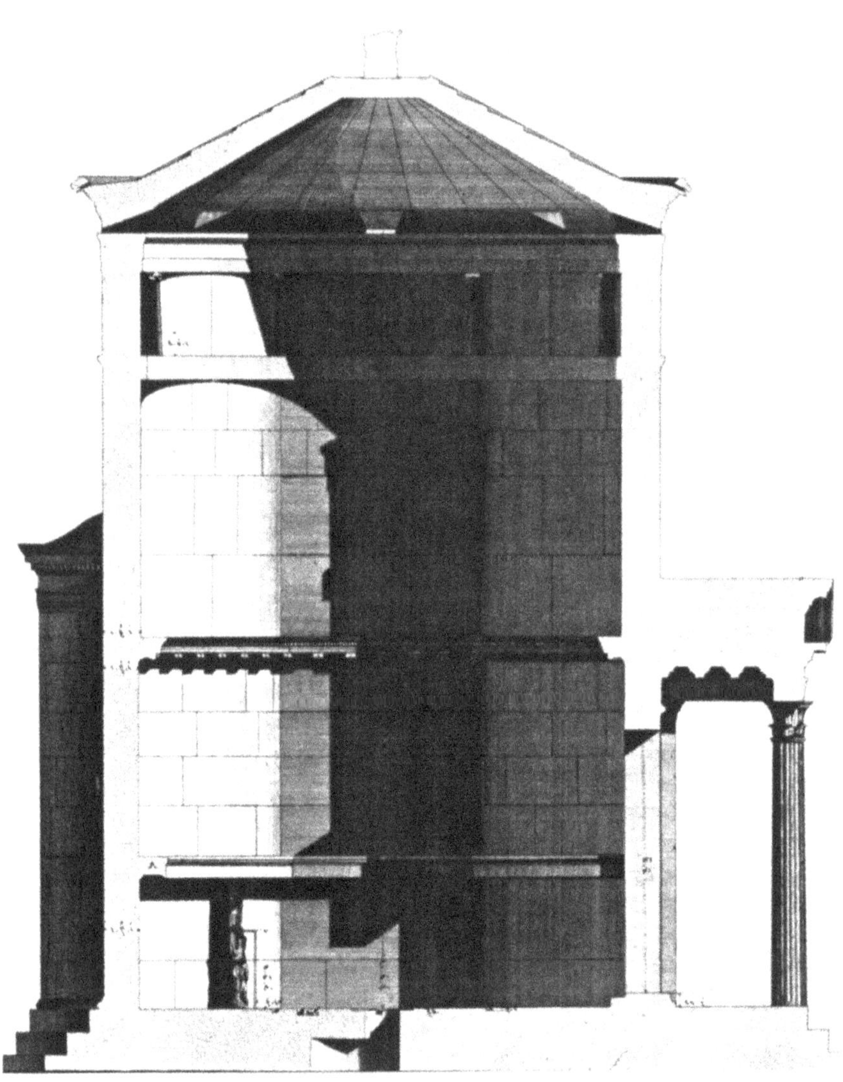

4. Reconstruction of the interior of the Tower by Stuart and Revett (1762)

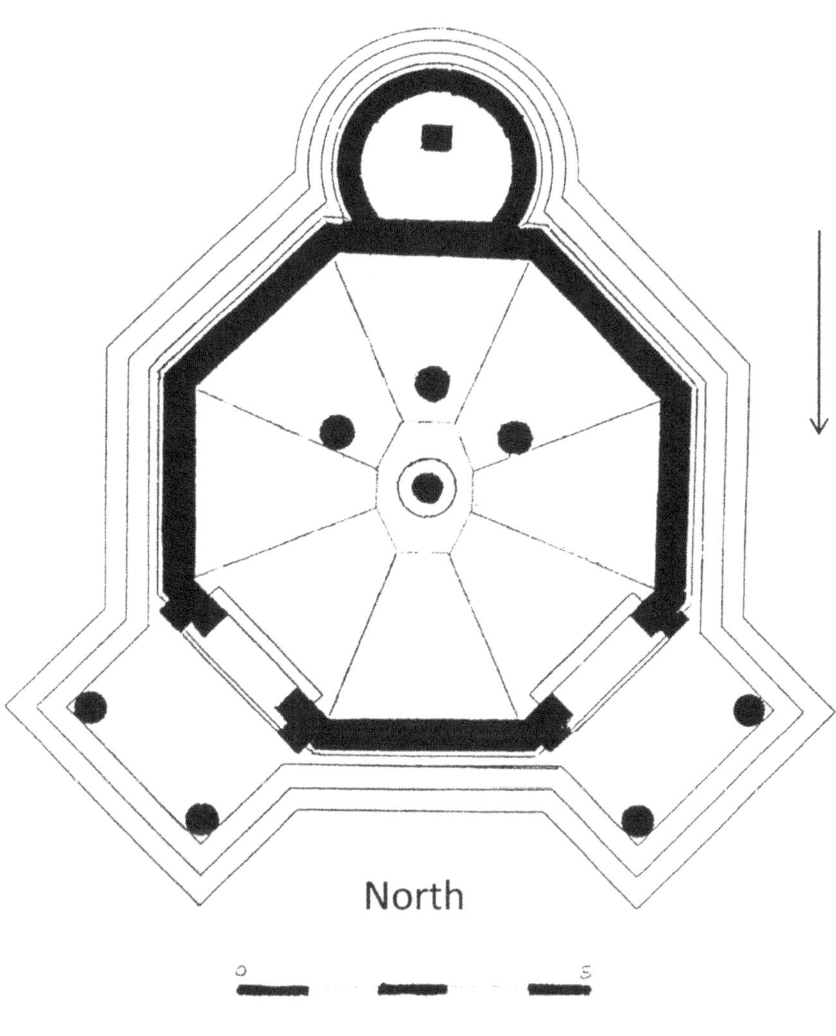

5. Floor plan of the Tower in the Hellenistic Period.

6a. The Tower and the arcuated wall viewed from the west through the Roman Agora.

6b. View of the arcuated wall on the south side of the Tower.

6c. The platform of the arcuated wall (at the right), which is built atop the crepidoma of the Tower's annex.

7a and b. Fragments of the front and west side of an entablature from one of the Tower's porches.

8a. The column shafts and the undamaged threshold of the northwest porch.

8b. The undamaged threshold of the northwest door.

8c. The worn threshold of the northeast door with cuttings for a smaller door that was installed in a subsequent period.

9. View of the Tower from the northeast showing the outline of the doorway.

10a. View of the Tower from the southeast, including the semi-circular annex on the south.

10b. View of the Tower from the southwest, including the semi-circular annex on the south.

11. View of the Tower from the west showing a window and an arched niche in Zone 3.

12. View of the interior of the Tower showing Zones 1–3 and the window in the northwest wall.

14a and b. Views of the cornice at the top of Zone 2.

13. View of the cornice at the top of Zone 1.

15. Remains of the mihrab in the southeast corner of the main chamber and a window that opened into the annex.

16. View of the cornice at the top of Zone 3, and an engaged column and the cornice at the top of Zone 4.

17a and b. Views of the domed ceiling and the upper walls.

18. View of the floor in the main chamber with cuttings from the various periods of occupation.

19. View of the small round holes that encircle the perimeter of the main chamber.

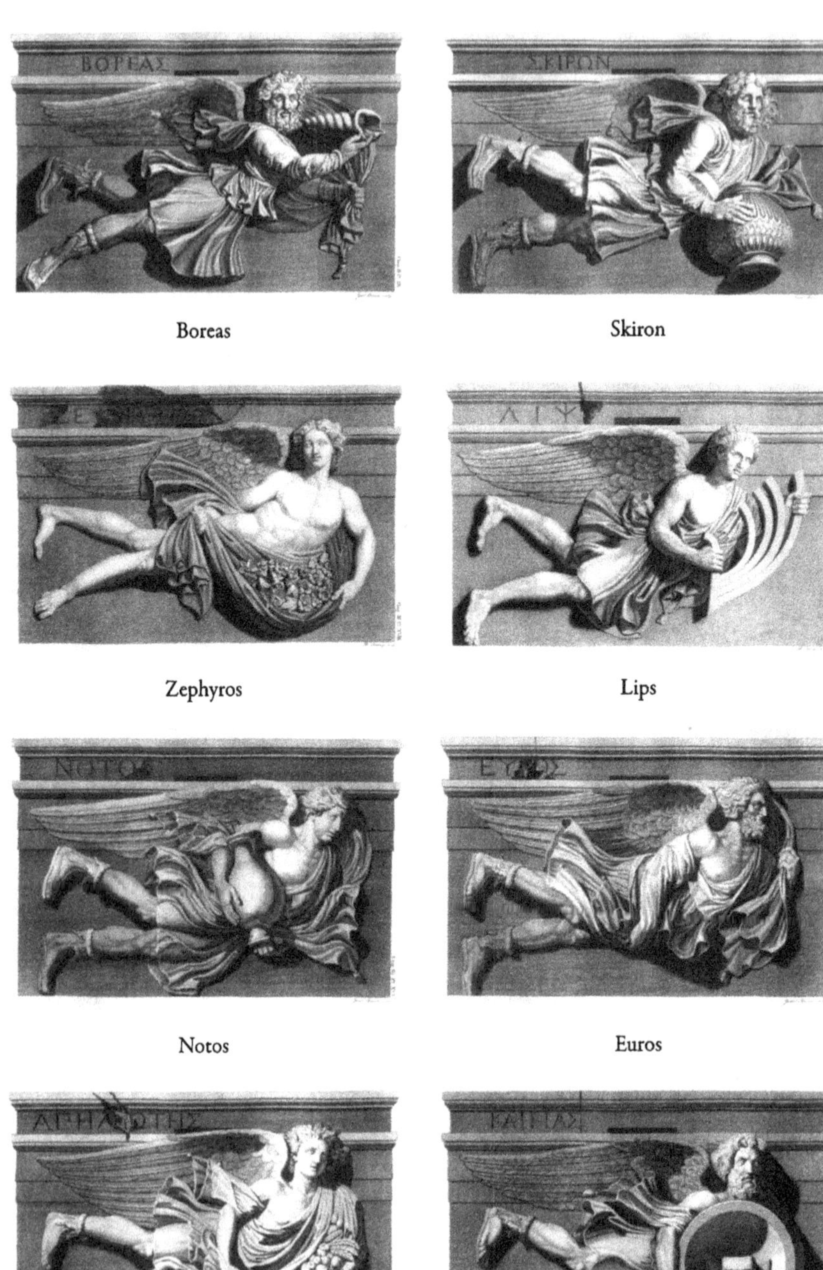

20. Drawings of the winds gods by Stuart and Revett (1762).

21a. Boreas

21b. Skiron and Zephyros

21c. Lips.

21d. Notos and Euros.

21e. Apeliotes.

21f. Kaikias.

22. Snaky-legged giant (in the center, being attacked by Artemis' dog) from the east frieze of the Pergamon Altar.

23. Bull-giant (at right) from the south frieze of the Pergamon Altar.

24. Amazonomachy frieze from the Temple of Artemis at Magnesia (south side, Block 19 P).

25. Amazonomachy frieze from the Temple of Artemis at Magnesia (south side, Block 27 P).

26. Male figure wearing *embades* with pronged *piloi* (at right) from the Telephos frieze on the Pergamon Altar.

27. Reconstruction of the Pharos at Alexandria.

28. Lysicrates Monument, Athens.

29a. Reconstruction of an anaphoric disk by Noble and Price.

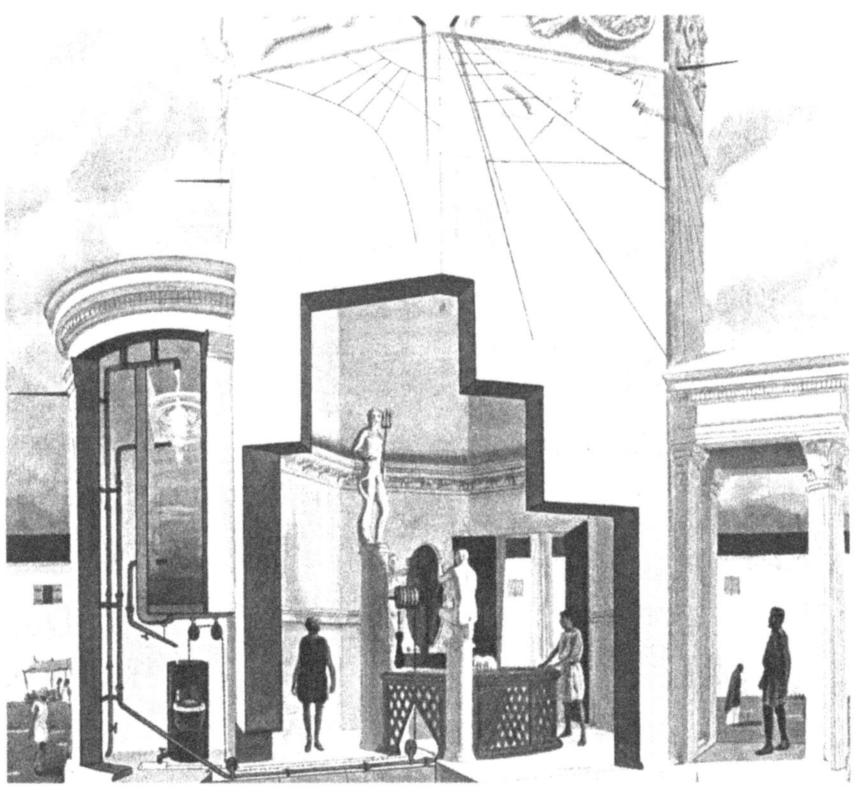

29b. Reconstruction of water clock with an anaphoric disk inside the Tower by Noble and Price.

30. The Farnese Atlas (with celestial globe) in the National Archaeological Museum, Naples.

31. Nike of Samothrace in the Louvre Museum, Paris.

32. View of the doorway into the annex and the water pipe channels cut into the floor of the main chamber during Roman renovations.

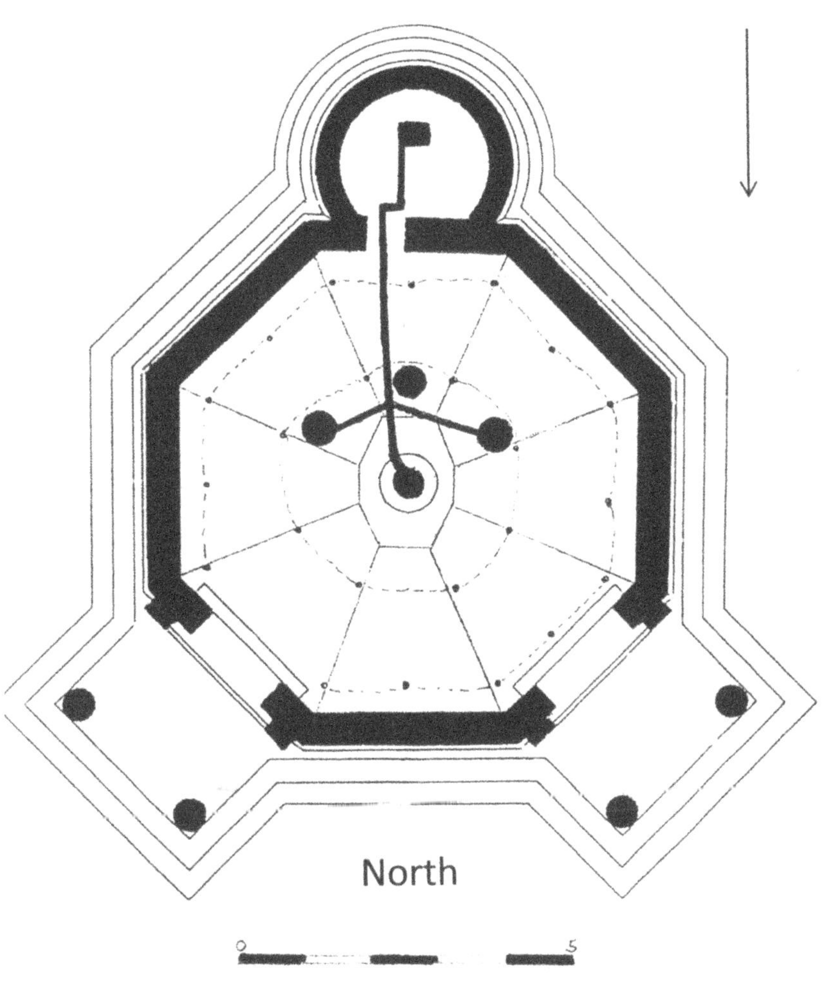

33. Floor plan of the Tower in the Roman imperial Period.

34. Small Latin cross carved into the east interior wall of the Tower's main chamber.

35. Fragmentary remains of a Byzantine wall painting at the top of Zone 2 in the Tower's main chamber.

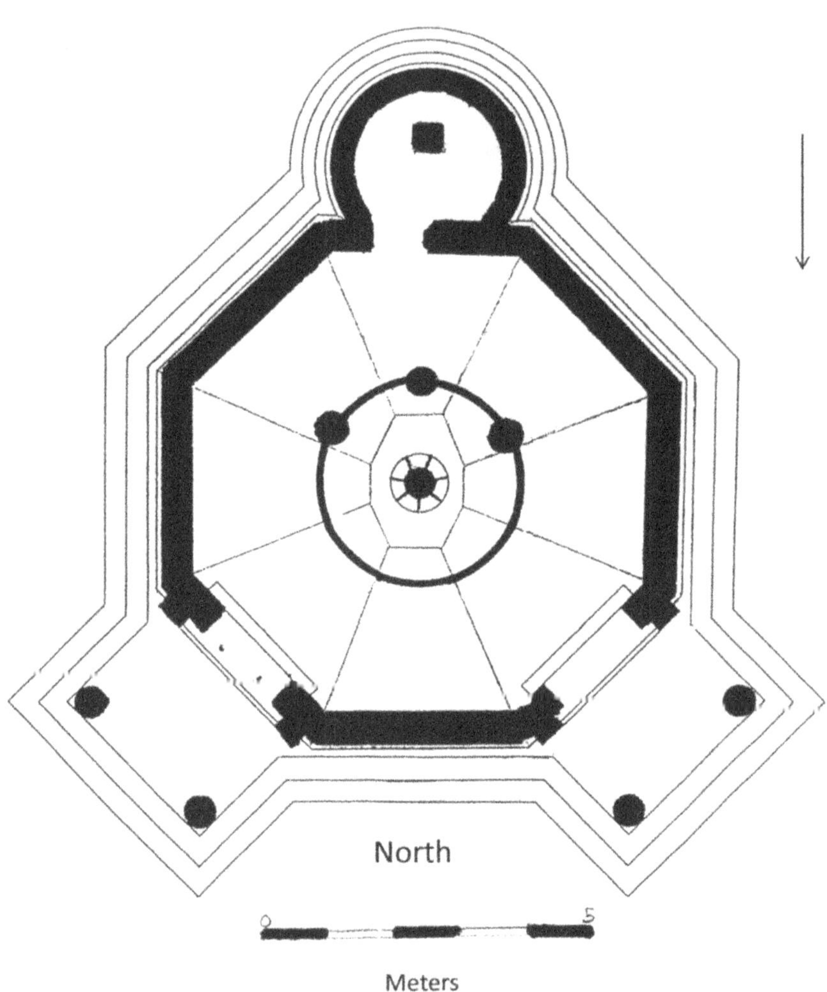

36. Floor plan of the Tower as a Christian martyrium.

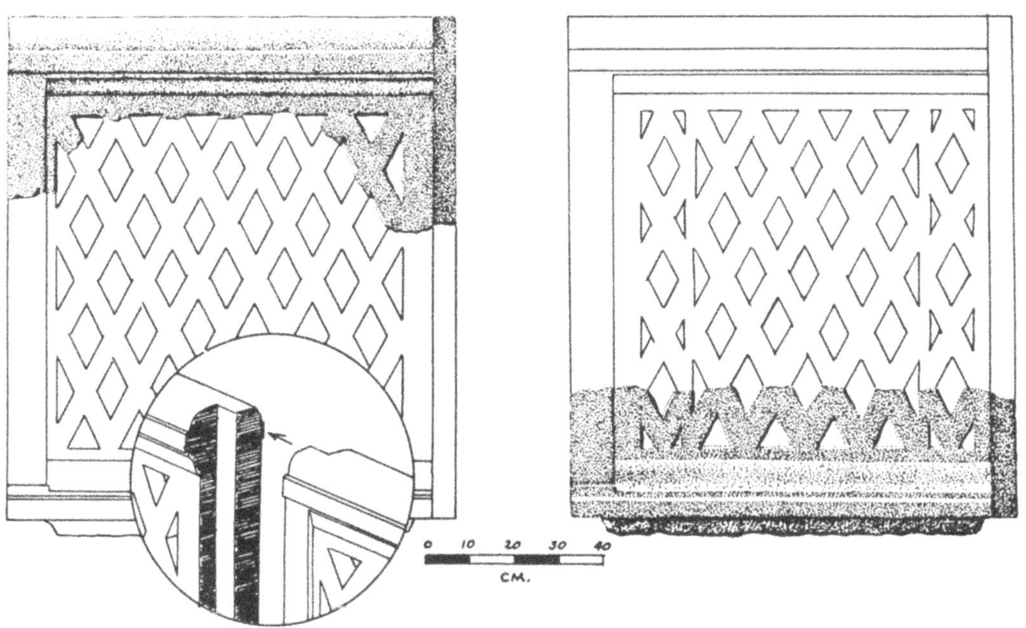

37. Reconstruction of the balustrade from the interior of the Tower by Noble and Price.

38. Sketch of the interior by Richard Pococke (1745).

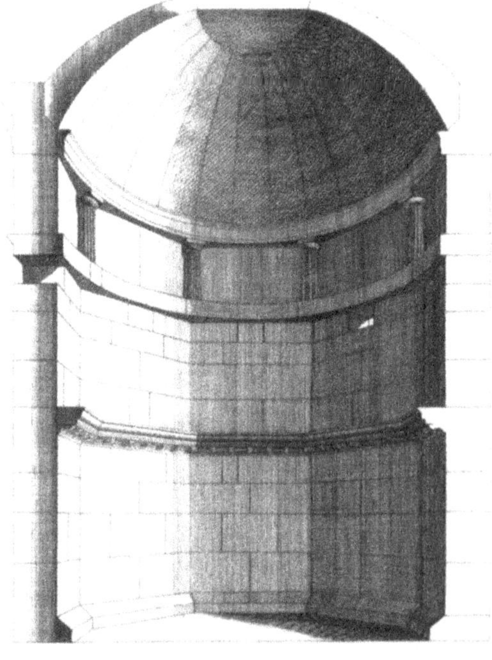

39. Sketch of the interior by Richard Dalton (1749).

40. Drawing of the Ottoman Tower viewed from the northeast by Stuart and Revett (1762).

41. Painting of the entrance to the Tower of the Winds as a dervish lodge by Edward Dodwell (1821).

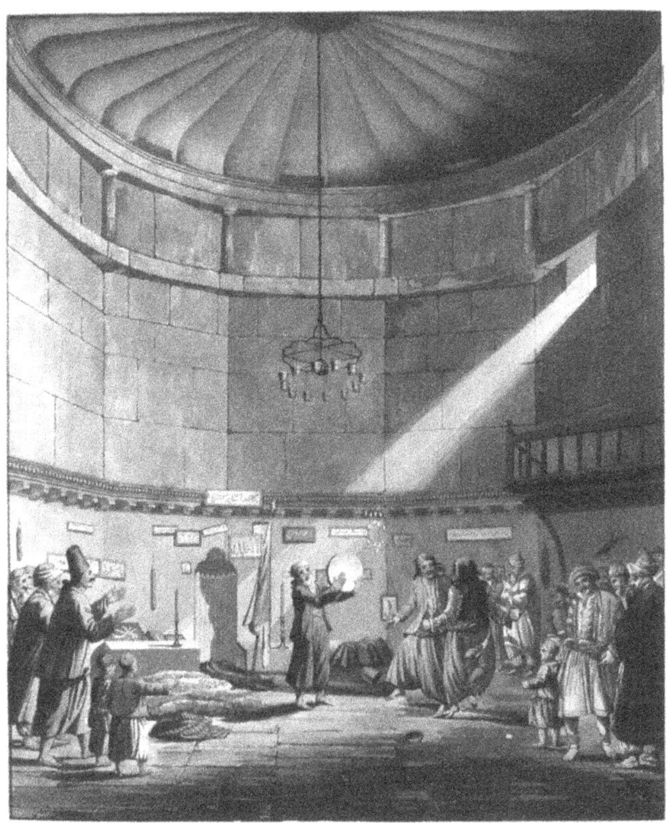

42. Paintings of the interior of the Tower of the Winds as a dervish lodge by Edward Dodwell (1821).

43. Drawing of the second mosque inside the Parthenon by J. D. LeRoy (1755).

INDEX

INDEX

www.ingramcontent.com/pod-product-compliance
Lightning Source LLC
Chambersburg PA
CBHW080919100426
42812CB00007B/2325